4/2012
ACPL Laramie, WY
39092080804620
Buzzell, Colby.
Lost in America :

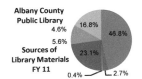

Lost in America

ALSO BY COLBY BUZZELL

My War: Killing Time in Iraq

‹   ‹   ‹   ‹   ‹   0   ›   ›   ›   ›   ›

Lost in America

* * * * * * * * * *

> > > > > A Dead-End Journey

Colby Buzzell

HARPER

An Imprint of HarperCollins*Publishers*
www.harpercollins.com

HarperCollins books may be purchased for educational, business, or sales promotional use. For information, please write: Special Markets Department, HarperCollins Publishers, 10 East 53rd Street, New York, NY 10022.

FIRST EDITION

Designed by Fritz Metsch

Library of Congress Cataloging-in-Publication Data

Buzzell, Colby.
  Lost in America : a dead-end journey / by Colby Buzzell.—1st ed.
     p. cm.
  ISBN 978-0-06-184135-4 (hardback) —ISBN 978-0-06-184136-1 (paperback) 1. Buzzell, Colby—Travel—United States. 2. United States—Description and travel. 3. United States—Social conditions—21st century. 4. Iraq War, 2003—Veterans—United States—Biography. 5. Men—Identity. 6. Fatherhood—Psychological aspects. I. Title.
  E169.Z83B89 2011
  956.7044'3—dc22

                                        2011012889

11 12 13 14 15   OV/RRD   10 9 8 7 6 5 4 3 2 1

For my mother

"If you are going through hell, keep going."

WINSTON CHURCHILL

Contents

INTRODUCTION

> *"I feel there is a universal sense amongst our*
> *generation that everything has been said and done.*
> *True. But who cares. It could still be fun to pretend."*
>
> KURT COBAIN

Putting my own personal feelings aside on Kerouac and the Beats, I enthusiastically agreed to this assignment to "Retrace Kerouac's footsteps and paint a contemporary portrait of America. A love letter to Kerouac." Now I could start this off by crafting a predictable segue into a nauseating tribute to Kerouac, offering some soulful reason for writing this book, or rambling about how I'm on a mission of self-discovery.

Like hell I am.

Times are hard, and right before I left their upper-floor midtown Manhattan office, after I'd shaken their hands and told them all thank you, that they'd all made a great decision and how I couldn't wait to start, one of them asked me if there was anything at all that would prevent me from doing this assignment for them. I paused, thought about that for a second, and then I lied. Shaking my head, I told him no, that there wasn't.

With a smile he said, "Good."

I smiled back.

Life takes its turns, and after purchasing an American classic off some stranger, I filled the tank, lit a cigarette, thought about Kerouac for a second, then thought about something else, put the car in gear, and headed off toward the opposite coast. Destination? East.

I don't write love letters.

Fuck that, and fuck Kerouac.

•

On my flight back home to San Francisco I began to worry at length about how in the world I was going to pull this one off while at the same time I was suffering from a huge migraine. I asked myself over and over again what in the world I'd just gotten myself into when, out of nowhere, I started thinking about the time growing up where I would hold my mother's hand as she walked me to school each morning. Recalling this time in my childhood, more specifically this one particular memory, seemed to calm me and make the road ahead less daunting.

The elementary school I attended was located only a couple blocks away from our house. I was either in the first or second grade at the time and my lunch box like always would be packed with a meal she had carefully prepared for me. She believed the Rambo lunch box I had wanted was too violent, so I had a G.I. Joe one instead. For some reason I have no memory of socializing with any of my classmates, none. Most of what I remember is sitting at my desk with my Beatles haircut (which my mother literally used a bowl to cut) wondering what in the hell was going on, and other assorted thoughts that seem much more important as a kid. What if the school was a spaceship and it launched and we all got to go into outer space? An elephant in the backyard would be cool. Cheerios with soda instead of milk: yum or gross? I want to be a professional bike racer and pedal really fast. What if I had every single toy that was ever made, do you think that's possible? Would they all fit in my room?

Always feeling off in my own world at recess, I'd keep myself company just walking around with my thoughts, head down, every now and then picking up a rock to see what kind of bugs were underneath or studying some flower growing in the grassy field bordering the school-yard.

One day the bell rang, indicating the end of recess. While all the other kids frantically ran back to class, I didn't. I saw no reason to. I just stood there out on that grassy field dumbly, watching. One by one doors began closing and silence filled the playground.

After a couple long minutes just standing there, waiting, I realized no one had noticed my absence back in the classroom. So I left.

I casually walked off campus, making my way down a couple of the suburban residential side streets, looking at the lawns and houses I passed. When I reached the nearby grocery center, I stood there and watched people pull up in their cars, park, enter the grocery store, leave. None of the adults seemed to notice me, or the fact that I wasn't at school. I slowly walked over to a nearby park, where there was a playground. I didn't play in it for whatever reason, though I remember just staring at it. Leaving, I headed down a busy street with cars thundering by. An enormous black van pulled up. After studying me for a bit, the lady driving told me to get in. I saw no reason not to.

A mob of parents crowded around once we arrived back at the school, one of the adults in this crowd a particularly frantic Korean lady. It was my mother. When she saw me exit the lady's van, her panic turned to a smile of relief and a warm hug. The crowd dispersed and my mother, after thanking them, grasped my hand tightly and walked me home.

Surprisingly she didn't yell at me at all, and I wasn't punished. Instead all she did was tell me never to do that again, that it scared the heck out of her, the other parents, and the teachers, that they had all feared the worst: that I'd been kidnapped or that "something bad happened" to me. All of this confused me. I nodded back, promising that I would never wander away again.

But I love grime, alleys, and alcohol. I'm an alley cat, I like to wander. It's not really any more complicated than that.

CHAPTER ONE

Rendezvous with Destiny

"I think it's a mistake to ever look for hope outside of one's self."

ARTHUR MILLER

That's it? *That's* the fucking speech that I flew all the way across the country to see? I could have YouTubed that from home, I'd be a lot fucking warmer if I had. Witness history, my ass. The only thing I'm witnessing here in D.C. is me freezing my ass off.

Not only did I desperately need to work more positive thinking into my life, but while trapped there, I also realized that had I YouTubed the speech from the comfort of my own room instead of making the effort to be one of many in attendance, I would have missed out on witnessing the behavior of the sea of people all around me. While just minutes before I had, dare I say, been somewhat moved by the thousands of miniature red, white, and blue flags proudly being waved around me, I was now watching as one by one they made their way onto the ground, carelessly tossed like cigarette butts, scattered all around. There they lay, discolored with dirty footprints, torn apart by the trampling masses. Nearby, trash cans overflowed with discarded flags. I noticed a young girl, maybe kindergarten age, collecting up these flags that had been thrown down into what was now mud.

Though I never made the rank of Boy Scout, I belonged at one time to the Webelos ("We'll Be Loyal Scouts"), later joining the Cub Scouts. I remember being taught that our nation's flag should never touch the ground. If that was to happen, it should be burned.

That thought was interrupted only by something far more shocking, the loud shout of a T-shirt hawker: "SALE! Fifty percent off!"

This guy looked like a big fan of all-you-can-eat buffets, waddling around with two arms full of those "Hope" T-shirts so en vogue just minutes before, now downgraded to the discount bin. I followed him for a bit, seeing that no one was buying. Nobody cared. Everybody had theirs already. Though I was tempted to purchase a "My President Is Black!" T-shirt, I couldn't see myself rocking a shirt with a politician on it, so I passed on the deal. Even at 50 percent off.

Speakers lined the National Mall, and while standing around midfield I heard a loud noise that sounded as though somebody had pulled the plug. On the big-screen televisions also lining the Mall, I could see our new president and vice president happily waving good-bye while Marine One, the presidential helicopter, lifted off above them with our old commander in chief.

The exodus, not unlike the one you see at a baseball game in the latter innings once everyone thinks they know who's won, hoping to beat traffic, seemed premature. As everyone worked their way toward the exit, the majority seemed oblivious to this moment, the handoff of our country.

Watching Marine One fly over me, I decided it was time for me to leave as well. The Bush years had come to a close.

Thanks to my experience as an infantryman in the army, where I would go for long stretches with everything I needed strapped to my back, I now prefer to travel light. Everything that I would need for my trip across the country was stashed away inside my backpack: three sets of clothes, laptop, camera, various battery chargers, pens, notebooks, that first copy of *On the Road*, purchased so many years ago, and . . . that's pretty much it. Slowly making my way to the Greyhound bus station, eager to begin the leg of my journey up to Lowell, Massachusetts, with the perspective on travel that can only be gleaned from hours of recycled air and the knowledge that the guy next to you didn't need to show any sort of identification before boarding, I pull out my cell phone to see whether I had any reception. I did, and there was a text from my sister.

•

Back home, my mother's hair was thinning. Many times while I was visiting her she'd remove her hat to show me the effects of the chemo, soon after breaking down, sobbing uncontrollably. There was nothing I could do or say.

Before I left for D.C., I had to wait around for the test results from her latest MRI. That particular MRI was to determine whether or not the chemo was working, whether or not the cancer was spreading. If the cancer spread, I was to call my publisher in New York and notify them of my mother's condition, which at that point they were totally unaware of, and kindly ask to postpone my trip across America for a bit. If they didn't grant me an extension, I'd be fucked, but not as fucked as my mother.

The results of the MRI came back, and miraculously the cancer did not seem to be spreading, which meant that my mother had some time left on this planet. No one knew how long, but we were all hopeful that it would be a very long time. Thus, I was able to hit the road. The plan was to finish the assignment, afterward spending as much time with her as possible.

But this decision wasn't easy, nor was it guilt-free. My mother had cancer. What if she couldn't beat it, and what if she passed away shortly after I came back, or even while I was away? I would have lost all that time I could have spent with her. On the other hand, if I didn't leave soon, I wouldn't be able to meet my publisher's deadline. What to do, what to do . . .

Earth to Colby: What's more important, you moron? Your book, or your mother?

The book.

What in the hell was I thinking? My mother had always stressed the importance of family. She had always said that there wasn't anything more important than that, though at this point, she also stressed the importance of health insurance. She would tell me that without health insurance, thanks to her condition, my father would be bankrupt right now, living in a world of shit. She'd have forever felt responsible for hurting the family in that way.

After receiving the results of the MRI, I asked my mother whether I should stay or go. Lying there in the hospital bed, of course she told me I should go, as I knew she would. I was still conflicted, which she sensed. With her plastic hospital bracelets wrapped around her shrinking wrists, she reached out and held my hand. I remember her hand feeling warm and soft, like an old washcloth soaked in hot water, as she told me again that I should go. I should go, and follow my dreams, and not worry about her; she'd be fine, and we'd get to hang out again plenty when I got back.

With a smile, she thought out loud and envisioned the entire family, now somewhat spread out, together again. She seemed to glow at that thought, even talking of a vacation for all of us once I returned, "somewhere nice."

But the text message I received now from my sister said that my mother wasn't doing well, deteriorating by the day, and that I should strongly consider coming back home.

I booked a flight back for the following day, and called my father to get an update on the situation. I could hear my mother in the background, crying loudly from the pain, while hauntingly moaning, "Help me," over and over again, followed by my name.

CHAPTER TWO

Take as Needed for Pain

> *"It was written I should be loyal to the nightmare of my choice. I was anxious to deal with this shadow by myself alone—and to this day I don't know why I was so jealous of sharing with anyone the peculiar blackness of that experience."*
>
> JOSEPH CONRAD,
> *Heart of Darkness*

The voice message I had received from my father months before had a mixed tone of urgency, concern, and confusion, which struck me as a bit off, since my father had never shown any of those emotions around family. When I called him back, he got straight to the point, letting me know that my mother was sick, really sick, and that he was going to need to take her to the hospital. They were heading to Mount Eden Hospital in Castro Valley.

At this point in my life, I don't live very far from where I grew up, a fairly quick BART ride from San Francisco. When I arrived at the hospital, my father and sister, who had flown up from Orange County, were with my mother, who was in tremendous pain, screaming and crying as though her limbs were being pulled away from her. I got there just in time to witness this horrific scene, as the nurses whisked her into a room to inject her with morphine. I watched the nurse administer the medication, my eye following the bottle, following the nurse's hand, curious where they'd set it. I found myself wondering whether they could write it off as a loss, which reminded me that I have some serious mental problems.

As the pain went away, a beautiful smile spread across my mother's face, which made me also smile. My mother was now on drugs, which was a strange thing to witness. I thought back to each time she had accused me of being on drugs, when I hadn't been. I thought back to each of those other times that I was in fact high as a kite, but she hadn't suspected a thing as I quickly walked past her through the kitchen on my way up to my room.

My sister was also there. "Why are you smiling, Mom?" she asked.

My mother smiled beautifully. "The baby," she said.

"What are you talking about, Mom?" my sister asked. "What baby?"

My mother pointed to the corner of the room. "Cute baby," she said. And with that same smile, she said, "Colby's baby."

My mom's on drugs, and in more ways than one she was now seeing things.

Later the next day, while waiting in the hospital's main lobby—which, a few hours in, began to aggravate me, as I couldn't understand why a hospital would ever furnish its lobby with such an uncomfortable sofa since no one really spends a long period of time in a hospital lobby for any reason other than something traumatic—a doctor wearing a crisp white coat appeared. He matter-of-factly informed us all—my Korean aunts had joined us at this point—that my mother, who was somewhere in one of the top-floor hospital rooms above, had cancer, and that, worse yet, it was terminal cancer. On average, people with this same type of cancer generally had about six months to live. Once delivering this bit of information, he did an about-face and stiffly walked away.

My father, always stoic, broke down in tears. I needed a smoke.

My sister followed me. As she stepped outside, tears mixed with mascara running down her face, she asked me, "What are we going to do?"

I exhaled, telling her that I didn't know. Furrowing my brow, I wondered why I wasn't crying.

It was late evening now. As I stared up at the cold concrete hospital in front of us, many of the rooms lit, I thought about how my mother was inside one of those rooms, dying. Listening to the low hum of automobiles passing on the nearby freeway, I had a pretty good idea of what I needed to do now. I needed to move back home to be with my mother as much as possible. For once in my life, I would try to be the son that I never had been. Once she passed away, I would hit the road permanently, just wander. Fuck it. What's the point now, you know? There is none. A bit dramatic and over-the-top, but these were the thoughts running through my mind as I stood there with my sister, through smoke and tears.

•

Having returned from D.C., I went to my parents' house. My parents still lived in the home I'd more or less grown up in, a beige stucco two-story, in a style characteristic of many California homes built in the early 1980s, complete with three-car garage. My father had worked hard to save money for a house in a low-crime suburb with good schools, white pickups showing up weekly to keep the lawns manicured; the ideal location to raise a family.

When I arrived, I saw that all of my mother's hair had now disappeared completely as she lay asleep on a hospital bed in the living room where we'd spent so many years living, covers pulled up to keep her warm.

Even in sleep she appeared to be in pain. My father did too, though a different kind of pain, an emotional pain; you could tell that this was also taking a heavy toll on him physically. He was going through hell, and he looked the part. He walked with a slight limp, had enormous bags under his bloodshot eyes, and commented that the last time he was this sleep-deprived was back in Vietnam.

He had always been a strong man, and his spirit was not entirely broken; he still clung to the hope that my mother would somehow pull through all of this. That, I think, kept him going.

I never said a word about it, but I was somewhat more skeptical. I didn't like what I was seeing one bit, and by now, a part of me wished my mother dead. I wished her dead because, well, she's my mother. The lady who'd walked me to school every morning, holding my hand. You only get one biological mother, and for many, including myself, nobody will ever love you as unconditionally. I no longer wanted to see her suffering the way that she was—a slow, torturous death leaving her in severe, unrelenting pain. I wanted it all to end.

Absolutely exhausted, my father explained to me my job for that evening. After that, he slowly walked upstairs to the room he had once shared with my mother. I pulled a chair up to my mother's bed and sat there. Waiting, listening to my mother's lungs expand and contract silently and slowly after every breath while she slept.

For some reason, the cancer, or maybe the chemo, was now making my mother feel that she always had to urinate. Whenever she needed to go to the bathroom, my job would be to lift her out of bed, place her onto her wheelchair, cover her with a blanket, roll her to the bathroom down the hall, lock the wheels, lift her out of the wheelchair in a bear hug, place her in front of the toilet, and, while holding her with one arm, use my free hand to pull down her sweatpants, and then seat her on the toilet. From there, I'd take a seat on the wheelchair outside the bathroom, waiting for her to finish; sometimes it was a couple minutes, sometimes nearly an hour. When she was finished, I'd have to wipe her off, and if she needed new adult diapers, I'd change them for her. Then we'd run through the same motions in reverse, get her back on the bed, straighten her out, and pull the covers up to keep her warm.

My father had been doing this for the past several nights, and it was now my turn for the next several days.

Every time I had to wipe off my mother after taking her to the bathroom, I couldn't help but think that this was not the way it's supposed to be. I vaguely remember being a toddler, yelling for her whenever I was finished taking a shit on the potty, and she would arrive to wipe my ass. It vexed me to have it all turned around now. Seemed wrong. Here I was, years later, wiping her ass.

For the pain, I gave my mother two generic Vicodin every forty-five minutes. Two for her, one for me. Why they didn't give her something stronger than Vicodin, I'll never know. Vicodin hardly did anything for me anymore, even when I mixed it with alcohol, as I have unfortunately often done.

At night, while my mother was passed out, I'd watch television. They had cable, but I was surprised to find that there's hardly anything to really watch late at night except paid infomercials, all promising a quick fix with little to no effort, solving every imaginable major problem afflicting your average American. If they can regrow hair, enlarge a penis, provide senior citizens with all-day erections, use bands of rubber to whittle away a tummy, pills to dissolve fat, first, what the fuck is wrong with these people and more importantly, why can't they come up with a cure for cancer?

I'd buy that.

·

The morning sun began to peek in through the windows, creeping across the white carpet my parents had installed after all of us kids moved out. I decided to leave the television on, turning it to one of those channels playing nothing but music, having found one playing only big-band music.

No idea what happened to it, but when I was growing

up, there was always a radio in the living room. Whenever my mother was folding clothes, or in the kitchen, she'd always have it on Magic 61, an AM radio station playing nothing but oldies, and a lot of big-band tunes. It was always set to that station, and as I got older, she'd get pissed off whenever I changed it to Live 105, the alternative rock station, angrily making me change it back. It's funny because I now love the music made during those early eras, the 1920s, '30s, and '40s. If somebody was to change my radio presets over to an alternative rock station, I'd react exactly as my mother had—pissed.

An old Glenn Miller song was playing, I forget which one, but it was one of his more somber numbers. Sitting by her bed, I could see my mother slowly coming to, not in pain, eyes opening. She asked what I was watching.

It was a near miracle to see her waking up calmly, as she often woke up in horror, head swiveling, frantically looking for my father, asking "Where is he?! I want to see him before I die!"

That morning, she didn't do that. She seemed to be just as relaxed as the melodies coming from the television, and for the first time in a long while, able to talk. I wanted to jump all over this opportunity, so I told her how I remembered that she used to listen to the big-band station on the radio all the time when I was a kid. She seemed surprised I could recall all this.

"You remember?" I told her I remembered a lot of things. She smiled, then sourly commented that today's music was "garbage," that she liked older music "much better."

I nodded in agreement, and the two of us, there in the living room, stopped talking, listening to that wonderful song together in silence.

Then out of nowhere she said, "I'm hungry."

She said it as the song ended, and another one came on, maybe Tommy Dorsey. I don't remember, since I was more stunned than anything by my mother's statement—she hardly ever ate. Lately she had only been able to stomach protein shakes, which we purchased in bulk at Costco, force-feeding her through a straw. So I got up quickly, heart rate going, and asked her what she wanted. She thought about it for a second, and then she said, "Miso soup." Okay, miso soup it is. Frantically, I wondered how in the hell to do this. I didn't know how to make miso soup; did we even have miso soup?

She told me to go over to the fridge, and that there I would find a jar labeled "Miso." From the bed, she gave me instructions on preparing it: Get a pot, fill it up with water, boil it. Dump a teaspoon of miso into the water. Easy enough. She then told me that she wanted tofu with it, so I quickly grabbed a pack of that from the fridge, chopped it up, and dumped it into the soup. While that was getting ready, I asked her whether she wanted anything else. She paused, and then requested a Korean pear. Again, from the bed, she instructed me to cut one into thin slices. While cutting into it, still in shock that all this was going on, I accidentally cut my finger. Drawing blood, I cursed. My mother asked what happened. While grabbing a napkin to wrap around my finger, I told her, "Nothing."

Blood seeping through the napkin, I brought the pear

over to my mother, who sternly gave me some constructive criticism on how I needed to concentrate more when doing things instead of moving too quickly. She ate her pear feverishly, asking for her soup. I brought it over, and while waiting for it to cool down, she asked me if I loved the girl I was with, who, I surprisingly discovered just days after the news that my mother had cancer, was now pregnant, several months along in carrying my son.

I said yes, with plans to remarry. My mother then told me that she knew she didn't have much time left, and that when she was gone, she wanted me to take care of the mother of my child, and my son, ensuring that he had everything that he needed, always, and to spend as much time with him as possible.

"Your father, he keeps everything inside—no good. You do same thing—no good, too." She then, again, stressed the importance of family and that nothing else really matters.

"Look at me, say I have no family. Then nobody care and help me. Who help me? No one. Family important."

While we talked, my father came downstairs to go to work. As he stepped into the living room to check in on us, he lit up, shocked at what he was seeing. My mother was talking! And eating! He couldn't believe it, and I was still having a hard time believing it myself. I knew he was thinking the same thing I was, that maybe she was on her way to a full recovery. Before leaving for work, he said something to me about how I should continue to talk to my mother, and do so more often, something I've been historically bad at doing. He threw in something about how it "seemed to work."

Before leaving, my father leaned over to kiss my mother good-bye. The garage door shut as my father was on his way to work, and it was once again just the two of us, my mother closing her eyes to rest.

.

As I felt my eyelids getting heavy and began to doze off, all hell broke loose. My mother started moaning in pain again, each moan more and more intense, every minute more turbulent. I was shoving Vicodin in her mouth, but could see that they weren't doing a damn thing. After popping a couple myself, I called my father and told him he should come home, it was time.

We moved her, crying in pain, into the car and left for the hospital. As we pulled out of the driveway, I stared at the house and remembered the first time we'd pulled up to it when we were moving in. My father, driving, called my Korean aunts, relaying the grim situation. He didn't go into much detail, though the severity of it was implied by his directness.

After assessing the situation, the doctor came to the decision that it was time for my mother to be in hospice. In Korean, my aunts explained to my mother what that would mean; seated in a wheelchair, sobbing, she bobbed her head up and down, indicating that she understood. That image, and the sounds I heard in that room, is permanently engraved in my memory. Aside from the doctor, I was the only one in that room not crying. I once again wondered what in the hell was wrong with me. I wasn't emotionless, but just stood there grimacing.

.

Both my sister and brother dropped everything to take the first available flight home. Now that hospice was involved, the entire family was to be home. My brother and I assigned ourselves to the rooms we'd grown up in, my sister slept next to my mother on her hospital bed there in the living room, my father on the sofa beside them.

After a short night of sleep, my sister woke me up. I could tell by the low look on her face and her tone that she didn't have good news. Solemnly, she told me, "Mom's not going to wake up. She went into a coma last night."

Walking downstairs, I entered the living room, where my mother lay, softly breathing. We all pulled up chairs from the dining table around her as my father contacted the hospice nurse and my Korean aunts.

Aunt Annie arrived first, the hospice nurse arriving soon after. She began to check my mother's vitals, lifting her eyelids, appraising her breathing pattern. With years of experience, she got to the point and told us all that whatever we had to say, we should say it now.

Looking at my mother lying peacefully in a coma, we asked how much time we had. She hesitated, as though she was withholding information, and just said, "Minutes," adding, "Maybe even less." Great.

The hospice nurse told us that despite being in a coma, my mother could hear us. She mentioned that she didn't think Aunt Suki and Halmoni—our Korean grandmother, who we lovingly referred to as "Harmony" while growing up—would make it in time, as they were coming from San Mateo. My father pulled out his cell phone, called them quickly to communicate the status, and then put the cell phone up to my mother's ear. From my seat there, I could hear a bunch of crying and Korean coming loudly through the cell phone, and since I don't speak a word of Korean, asked Aunt Annie what was being said. She told me that Halmoni was telling my mother to hold on for her, and not to go until she got here. They were a good forty-five minutes away. We again asked the nurse if they'd make it in time, and she told us probably not.

Defiantly, Aunt Annie told her, "She'll still be here. You don't know my sister, she'll hold on for her mother, she will."

One by one we started talking to my mother, who at this point was just barely breathing, like a fish out of water, each breath looking as if it would be her last. We all started telling stories, sharing memories that we had of her, and out of nowhere my aunt brought up how she remembered that when my mother was pregnant with me, all she wanted was miso soup. I stood up in my seat. I never knew that, nobody had ever mentioned it. I could barely believe it.

My father leaned over the woman he had married some thirty years earlier, put his hand on hers, and with tears slowly making their way down his face, dropping, absorbing into the fabric of the blanket covering her, said, "Honey, I love you, it's okay to let go. I love you so much, almost too much. You put up a good fight. It's okay to let go."

I was off in my own world, taking this all in, when suddenly my sister exclaimed, "Oh, my God, Mom can hear us! Look!"

There was a single tear welling beneath her eye, which slowly rolled down her cheek. At that moment, the front door opened, and my mother's sister, mother, and brother, who had flown all the way from South Korea, burst into the house. My mother had held on for her mother. A few minutes later, right there in the living room, in the house we had grown up in, her entire family around her, she quietly stopped breathing.

•

Many times early on at the hospital, when my mother was first diagnosed, she would simply say, "Talk to me." And I'd always be at a loss for words, never knew what to say other than, "Hi, Mom," which would break her heart. Tears would pour from her eyes when she'd tell me that I needed to communicate with her more often, open up to her. As she became more ill, I tried my hardest to force myself to talk as much as I could, but there will forever be a part of me that hates myself for not doing so sooner.

One of the many things I learned about my mother during this time spent with her was that her father killed himself. I arrived at the hospital one evening wearing a scarf around my neck, since it was a bit chilly. A scarf around my neck was a bit out of character for me, which caused her to take suspicious note of it and inquire as to my reason. Not thinking anything of it, I told her I had come across it in some shop, put it on, liked it, liked the price, liked the color (it was gray), and so went ahead and purchased it.

She nodded, called me strange, which was normal, and then told me a story about her father, whom I knew next to nothing about. All I knew about him was that he was dead. Period.

The story began with her reminding me that they were poor, and needed money for food. One day, her father came home wearing a brand-new scarf around his neck. Upon seeing this, a battle ensued between him and my grandmother, Halmoni, who exploded, cursing him over his stupid scarf, since what they needed was money for feeding the family, not for scarves.

He tried to explain to her that it was fashion, and that he liked the scarf. I would imagine she didn't care for that at all, since men's fashion had very little to do with food. While listening to the story, I laughed at the thought of my Halmoni, all five feet of her, unloading on her husband like a caged pit bull at the mere mention of the word *fashion*.

I was taken aback by all this. When we were kids, she would tell us her father was up in heaven, or "happy mountain," whenever we'd asked about him. By the way she wouldn't say anything further, it was understood that we were never to bring him up.

But on this occasion, late at night in her room at the hospital, just the two of us, my mother told me more about her father. She told me he liked to drink, a lot, especially loved whiskey, and how he also loved to gamble and chase women. So far, he sounded pretty cool to me. When she sensed this, she tried to extinguish that thought by explaining that due to his behavior, she and her family grew up poor, very poor, and that her mother, who had grown up rather well off, had to raise the entire family by herself while her husband blew all his money on booze and gambling, leaving nothing for the family he had abandoned.

To emphasize this point, she told me that in her village in Korea, the kids would have to bring money to their teachers every now and then to pay for school. If you didn't have any money for the teacher, the teacher would beat you in front of the entire class. The ruler smacked hard on her hands, and the worst part of it all, she told me, was that the other kids would tease her for not having money for school. My mother also had stories of being very young and her mother sending her out into their village many times to find her father and to tell him that the family had no food, and needed money. Many times he'd be drunk or with another woman when my mother would find him. She'd yell at him for money, and every time he would claim to not have any, sending her home empty-handed.

Learning all this explained a lot to me; why my mother always hated my drinking, and why she always made sure we had everything that we needed. She always made sure we had nice clothes, food on the table, and everything that we could possibly need for school. It also explained why, while growing up, my mother had always had a special place in her heart for my friends being raised by single mothers. She'd always ask me about them more than about anyone else—how they were doing, how their mothers were doing, always a bit of sorrow for them in her voice.

Now I knew why.

Decades after abandoning my mother's family, my grandfather wrote each member a letter indicating that he was getting older, and had no family, and no one to help take care of him. He was all alone, and planned to kill himself.

He had determined how he was going to kill himself, where he was going to kill himself, and where he was to be buried. He even planned the exact date on which he was going to do it. When that date arrived, sure enough, he did it.

My mother leveled her steady gaze toward me, and told me that when she went back to Korea several years ago, her first visit since leaving shortly after I was born, she left a bottle of whisky and a deck of cards on her father's grave.

·

> The writer must learn how to handle the problem of loneliness. For writing is a lonely profession. It is one road a man must walk by himself.
>
> ISABELLE ZIEGLER,
> *Creative Writing*

Much had changed since I first attempted to set off on my mission. The Obama administration was well under way, my mother had passed, I was now remarried and preparing for the birth of my son. Determined to pick up where I had left off, I reread *Travels with Charley* in addition to *On the Road*. When I first read *Travels with Charley* years back, I thought it was about an old guy wanting to reacquaint himself with the country that he had written about so much throughout his career. This second time reading it I'm thinking the book was just an excuse for

Steinbeck to get away from his wife for a bit. All he had pretty much written prior were novels and works of fiction; then, all of a sudden, he decides one day to go off and write nonfiction, a first-person narrative about traveling across America? Yeah, right. Sounds suspicious. What I could see happening is Steinbeck in his quiet room, door shut, surrounded by dusty woodwork, smoking another cigarette in front of his typewriter, trying to bang away on his *East of Eden* manuscript or something, constantly interrupted by his wife. "John, we need to run to the market. You think we could do that?" Or, "John, could you pick up some dog food for the poodle later on today, we're getting low. [*Sniff, sniff.*] Are you smoking again? You promised me you were going to quit after *Our Winter of Discontent*!" I could see John just losing it one day. I love her, but I need a fucking break! By golly, I know, my next book will be about me traveling. I'm going to tell her, "Sorry, babe, but I gotta hit the road for this one, the publisher wants me to discover America. Sorry. It's a publishing trend right now. *On the Road* did well, and they want me to do the same thing." Only a writer could get away with doing such a thing. John figured it out. "Now that she's bought that crap, I'm going to buy a camper, where I can totally drink and smoke all day and night without any interruptions at all, and I'll take the fucking poodle with me so that whenever I call her for the I-love-you phone call, I won't have to hear some long boring story that starts with, 'Guess what Charley did today?' This will be amazing."

It was heartbreaking to say good-bye to my wife whom I love dearly and my week-old son, tears were shed, but I'm not going to lie—there was this deep dark secret which I was keeping to myself, the one where I couldn't wait for this adventure to begin. The story gets worse. I'm leaving my wife and son to travel across the country for an uncertain duration of time, and what's more fucked up than that is that I'm secretly feeling in no rush to get back home again. And, by the way, I'm not making any of this up. As much as I wish it was, this book is not a novel.

Go ahead and write me off as an unlikable character. Trust me, I've been called far worse, and since I'm on a roll right now, truth be told, for me, experiencing life with a pregnant woman was no honeymoon (I don't care what anybody tells you, no trimester is any easier than another) in a tiny overpriced downtown San Francisco studio apartment in some crack-infested neighborhood, all while my mother was dying, has been one of the most challenging experiences of my life. Ever. Worse than war. I'm amazed I didn't blow my head off at some point. Really, I swear to God I am. Fuck what you see on television on channels like *TLC*, pregnancy is absolutely nothing like that. Those shows they air make pregnancy look fun. Pure joy. Sadly, it's not. Perhaps it was just my situation, but it was bloody hell. The fights, the feeling that I could do nothing right, the long lectures about not drinking and smoking, her saying, "I did it, why can't you?" The arguments, the wars about virtually everything and anything, the countless nights spent sleeping on the sofa, hearing those terrifying words, "I'm hungry," followed by a long monologue on weight gain, like it's the end of the world. And the Lamaze classes. How she wanted a doula, me asking, "What the fuck is a doula?" (Note: spell-check doesn't acknowledge what the fuck a doula is, either, but it's basically a companion offering support through pregnancy and birth.) How, after hearing her explanation, and why she felt she needed one, me telling her that we didn't need a doula, particularly not for FIFTEEN HUNDRED DOLLARS, and that I was the fucking doula. The yelling because I wasn't reading all of the pregnancy books she wanted me to read, and her blowing up when I made the mistake of casually telling her, "If you've read one, you've read them all."

I needed a break, and for my sins I finally got one.

One of the few promises I asked my wife to make to me prior to embarking on this journey of mine was that she never asked when I'd be coming back home, or "How much longer?" as I wasn't going to even attempt to answer those unanswerable questions while on the road.

"I'll be done when I'm done."

Nothing further.

CHAPTER THREE

The Path to Hell

"Who is the happier man, he who has braved the storm of life and lived or he who has stayed securely on shore and merely existed?"

HUNTER S. THOMPSON

They say you can never go home again, and leaving San Francisco, I was reminded of a story I once heard about a year and a half ago, told to me by a good friend, John, back when I was single, back when I was living the dream, living by myself, doing my thing, waiting for my most eligible bachelor nomination to arrive. John, who I have known since the second or third grade, was having his bachelor party out near Tahoe. I'm not a misogynist but at the time, I had no idea why in the world anybody in their right mind would want to be married, but whatever, I was going to the party.

We all pitched in and rented one of those cabins out in the woods, not too far from all of the casinos. Since I didn't own a vehicle at the time, I got a ride out there from another friend with whom I had also gone to elementary, junior, and high school, and who was also invited to the party. Though I've run into him over the years, the last time we really hung out together was back in high school, well over a decade ago. Since Tahoe was several hours away, we had plenty of time to catch up, and I could see that he was doing well. He owned a later-model pickup truck, had sporty sunglasses, looked well fed, and I could see his wedding ring glistening in the sun as he held both hands confidently on the steering wheel.

I came to find out he had purchased a house out in the suburbs, in the same town where we had both grown up, not too far from our old high school, and that he and his wife now had several kids. He was now a family man, and to keep the conversation going, I asked him what it was like being a father. I was curious; not because I wanted to start a family and move to the 'burbs or anything remotely psychotic like that, but because I lived in the city and none of my friends had any idea how to start a family. Gross, that's like, *so* suburban. He of course told me that being a father was great, the best thing to ever happen to him. "Yeah, it's a lot of work, but it's also rewarding to see them grow up," he said, and went on and on telling me how cool his three kids were, that what he was most looking forward to now was coaching his sons' baseball teams.

Safely arriving at our destination, hours before the strippers would arrive, the groom-to-be dropped by while I was at the keg refilling my red plastic Solo cup with yet another beer. He asked me how the drive had been, and said, "What'd you guys talk about?" So I told him that all we talked about was fatherhood. John shot me a look and asked what he had said about that. I took a sip, thought about it for a second, and told him that pretty much all he said was that it was cool.

"That's it?"

"Well, he told me that it was the best thing that had ever happened to him, and how wonderful it is; that he can't wait to coach baseball, shit like that. Why?"

John then told me a story that one day, not long before this, the wife of the guy who had driven me to Tahoe had called him, asking for a favor. This guy's birthday was coming up, and his wife had planned a huge surprise birthday party for him at the house. Everybody was going to be there, the whole family, kids, friends, all that. Since it was a surprise party, she asked John to take him out for a couple hours of golf beforehand, get him out of the house to make sure he wouldn't be around to spoil the surprise.

So they go out for a round of golf, and afterward they have a drink at the clubhouse. One drink turns into two drinks, two into three, and it's getting closer and closer to the time John has promised to return the birthday boy home. Each time he tells him that it's time to go, the guy doesn't want to leave. He keeps on saying, "No, let's just have one more drink, just one more, please? It's my birthday, and all I want is a drink at a bar." So they stick around for a couple more, and I guess his tolerance for alcohol isn't what it once was—being married with kids, he doesn't drink as much or as often as he'd like to thanks to the ball and chain— and the next thing he knows, birthday boy is totally ripped and begging him not to take him back home. "Please, let's just stay here and drink, seriously, you have no idea what hell my life is! *I hate it!*" And starts talking about how easy all "you single guys" have it, how they can go out and do whatever the hell they want to, how he's fucking phobic of the thought of going back to his own house—*terrified*. John listens to him ramble on for a while about how difficult his life is now, married with kids, bills, mortgage, no time to himself, etc., finally telling him that he has things to do that day, that it's time to go. On the drive back to the house, the car is quiet. Once they get really close, the guy recognizes some of the cars parked on his street.

Drearily, he says, "Looks like my in-laws are here."

When John says, "That's great, they all probably came to see you on your birthday," he answers, "Not really. They're always over, and I'm *sick* of being around them. Don't get me wrong, I like them, they're good people but, *Jesus fucking Christ*, they are always *here*!"

Parked in front of his house, he refuses to get out of the car—"Let's go back and just have one more drink? *Please?* I don't want to go home, just one more, I *swear.*" John tells him that he can't, and all forlorn, our old friend mopes back to his house. Of course when he opens the door, there waits the surprise birthday party that his wife has so meticulously planned, thoughtfully assembling all the people most important to him, and a few who are not so important. He quickly sobers up, puts on a smile, and enters the party.

•

A week after I left San Francisco, tore up and hung over, I find myself slowly coming to in a dive motel somewhere in downtown Reno. Empty bottles littered the room. I got up, suit and tie still on from the night before, and made my way to the bathroom. Urinated, flushed, and turned to the sink. After splashing some cold water on my face, I filled my hands and drank. I stared at my reflection.

"You're not a loser. You're smart. People like you. You're not a failure. You're not as ugly as you look. Women find you attractive. Life gets better, it does. It really, really does. It can't get any worse, right?"

When I got done lying to myself, a guy who said he was from India checked me out. I threw on my ultra-dark sunglasses, exited the lobby, and with the heat pressing down upon me, made my way over to my mistress, patiently waiting for me a block away. I picked her up right before I left San Francisco. She's hot. Drop-dead gorgeous, beyond sexy in my eyes, and so far she's been pretty good to me. Wouldn't go so far as to say she's the love of my life, but I like her a lot. She's got style, old-school even, and as far as age goes, I guess she'd be considered a MILF—a 1964 Mercury Comet Caliente. She's desert tan, four-door, V-8, and, of course, American-made.

I got inside, inserted the key, and fired up the engine, somewhat relieved that she started. I let her run for a bit, lit up another smoke, put her in drive, and headed toward I-80, continuing to live the dream.

I had stopped by downtown Sacramento on my way east to Reno, but found that scene to be a bore, even though the uphill drive through the night across the Donner Pass, up and over the Sierra Nevada, is somewhat exciting, in a *Please, car, don't break down* kind of way. Shortly after leaving the Reno city limits, thanks to the Hot August Nights car show, I seemed to pass a broken-down classic every couple miles, so I was thankful for having made it this far.

The first casualty I passed was a '57 Chevy, hood up,

looking like it was having engine problems. The second was a 1950s-era pickup with steam coming from its engine due to a blown radiator. Minutes later the third looked to be a Chevy Nova with a blown tire, which reminded me that I didn't have a spare. I didn't have one because I like to travel light, and it's not like I know how to change a tire anyway, so why have one? Not only can I not change a tire, but I can't change the oil filter, nor can I tell you where the spark plugs are located. I know next to nothing about cars beyond turning them on, refueling them, and whether they look cool or not. That's it. I should have brought some Xanax. I couldn't stop thinking that maybe people were right; maybe this was a bad idea.

.

To help get my mind off these thoughts, I found myself thinking about Amelia. The more I thought about her, the more I wanted to pull off the road. Who's Amelia? I'll get to that later. Finally, when I got to Fernley, Nevada, I said fuck it, lit another cigarette, pulled off I-80, not so that I could jerk off in a gas station stall thinking about Amelia but to take a side road. I had a different route in mind and needed to double-check that I was taking the correct exit. The young girl working behind the counter informed me that I was on the right path, that this was it, the exit to U.S. 50, the "Loneliest Highway in America." I thanked her.

> "It's totally empty," says an AAA counselor. "There are no points of interest. We don't rec-ommend it." The 287-mile stretch of U.S. 50 running from Ely to Fernley, Nev., passes nine

towns, two abandoned mining camps, a few
gas pumps and the occasional coyote. "We
warn all motorists not to drive there," says the
AAA rep, "unless they're confident of their
survival skills."

LIFE MAGAZINE, DESCRIBING NEVADA'S U.S.
50 AS THE LONELIEST ROAD IN AMERICA,
July 1986

Having, or pretending to have, a death wish can at
times be quite fun. If nothing else, it sure does make life
a bit more entertaining. Putting my foot in my mouth by
supporting another country overseas that, in turn, supports
terrorist organizations, I fill the Caliente's tank with some
premium 92 octane. For whatever reason, when I started
her up, the fuel gauge read empty. That's odd, I thought.
Ignoring the minor inconvenience of a busted fuel gauge,
I continued on my mission. Giddy with anticipation of the
unknown, I drove for a bit on 50, maybe thirty miles, arriving in a small town called Fallon, where I pulled in to
a Walmart parking lot to purchase some goodies for the
road, including one of those red five-gallon gas cans. When
I got back to my car, I placed the key in the ignition and
turned it. Nothing. I turned it again while pumping on the
gas. Nothing. Did this a couple more times, then finally
pulled the key out of the ignition, kind of sitting there for
a moment thinking about what the hell I was going to do
now. I decided to insert and turn the key one last time, and
the engine started up.

I lit another cigarette. While still parked, I let the

engine run and thought long and hard about what to do next. Do I attempt this? Or do I turn around and get back on I-80 so that when she does break down, I'll be a little closer to civilization? I watched people go about their everyday lives, parking their cars, entering Walmart, exiting, putting their bags into their trunks, driving off. I'm assuming that for many of them, this is the highlight of their day. There has to be more to life than that. *Don't be like them. Be a traveler, a man on the go!*

The sun was minutes from setting. I put the car in drive, exited the Walmart parking lot, made a right turn back onto U.S. 50, and headed east with the light fading behind me.

Within minutes, more or less immediately upon passing the city limits, I found myself alone in the middle of absolutely nowhere with nothing but brown land spread around me. I saw that I had no cell phone reception, which at first made me feel as if I had stupidly cast myself out to sea on some tiny boat, mistakenly having forgotten cigarettes and booze.

The drive was both peaceful, and terrifying. No sign of human life, nothing man-made. I enjoyed that immensely; it was like driving across a vacant planet. Then, like an acid flashback, that image sets my imagination off. Just like that, all the land around me turned ocean blue, and I once again started to think about Amelia.

My car stereo doesn't work, and with only the rumbling of the V-8 engine to keep me company, my thoughts were copiloting. I imagined myself wearing an aviator's cap, since this is what it must have been like for Amelia Earhart out over the Pacific. If she could do it, I could do it. My logic was, if my car broke down out here in the middle of nowhere, I could still survive, providing a pack of starved wild coyotes didn't find me first, or the person driving by to pick me up wasn't a serial killer. If Amelia's plane had suddenly stopped working, had her propellers just stopped, she was fucked. It's not like she could land the plane on the ocean, flip the hood, fix the radiator, and be on her way or wait for help. I could at least do that, minus the fixing part.

With the engine rumbling beautifully, I drove along for a bit. Once the sun finally set, there was absolutely no light at all inside my vehicle. Pitch-dark. I guess a fuse or something had blown, and right now, I couldn't see any of the meters on my dashboard. I had no idea how fast I was going, how low the oil pressure was, how high the engine temperature—not that either of those last two gauges worked to begin with—but more importantly, I could not see how much fuel I had in the tank, which I suspected was also broken.

I kicked myself for not purchasing a couple extra gallons of water and food provisions back at Walmart. I might wither from dehydration out in this vast nothingness, but it's a good thing I'd thought ahead so that I could do so with a cigarette hanging from my lip.

I sped by a lone deer on the side of the road that seemed tempted to jump out in front of me, and finally on the approaching horizon I saw signs of civilization. When I finally rolled into the small town of Austin, Nevada, I pulled into a lonely gas station and parked. Cramped from sitting so long, I limped inside. The lady working behind the counter had a huge smile on her face, her eyes fixed on my car.

"Did you drive that thing all the way here?" she asked with what I thought might have been a southwestern accent. I smiled back and told her that I had, and a bigger smile appeared on her face. She commented that the back fins of the car looked like wings, motioning with her hands that it looked like it could fly. If only she knew.

After a long drive like that, I needed a drink or two, or five or ten. So after filling up the tank I moved the car behind the gas station and, noticing the crickets chirping, made my way to the old bar across the street. Once inside, I saw that the bartender was an old-timer, and that there were only a couple people in there, all seated at the bar. I took a seat and ordered a shot of whiskey and a beer. I had my backpack with me, with my laptop and camera inside it; I brought it in with me to avoid losing anything if somebody should decide to break into my car.

I set my bag on the ground by my feet, and when the barkeep came back with my order, he asked where I was headed. I told him east.

"Hitchhiking?"

"No. Driving." The whiskey felt good.

"What you driving?"

"A 1964 Mercury Comet Caliente." The beer felt better.

"That'll do it."

.

As I left town the following morning, the road wound uphill for a bit, then straightened out, stretching as far as the eye could see, all the way to the horizon. At one point, looking into the rearview mirror, I could see exactly the same thing behind me as in front, nothing but the road just traveled. The sun was hot, the sky blue. Not a cloud in sight.

Operating radio or not, one of the many joys of long drives is allowing your mind to wander. Wearing my old desert tan BDU undershirt, I checked my reflection in the rearview mirror. A combination of my reflection and my surroundings reminded me that I could easily have been in Iraq right now, instead of doing this, which then brought Georgia into rotation, drifting once again back to Kerouac.

It was late 2003 when we crossed the Kuwait-Iraq border, driving all the way up through the middle of Iraq. We drove through Baghdad, spent some time in the Sunni Triangle, then moved on to Mosul, in the northern part of the country, near Syria. The path to that hell was very similar to the one I'm on now, except that there you'd pass by a burned-out Iraqi tank lying on the side of the road, .50 cal bullet holes slicing across the road. I remember even over there thinking of Kerouac, and how I was "on the road" in Iraq, feeling the excitement of an adventure while crossing the border into a combat zone, wondering whether or not I'd make it. Looking back, it might have been one of the happiest moments of my entire life.

Years later, once again a civilian living month-to-month in San Francisco, having thoughts of checking out, I received a lovely letter in the mail, causing me once again to think of Kerouac. The top left-hand corner indicated that it was from the U.S. Department of the Army, my previous employer. Inside were orders indicating that I had five weeks to report to Fort Benning, Georgia, "Home of the

Infantry," for in-processing. They stated that I'd be assigned to an infantry unit. Purpose: a return engagement to Operation Iraqi Freedom.

A couple days after receiving this letter, I took my parents out to dinner at an Italian restaurant in North Beach, my mother still in perfect health at this point. I remember telling my father that one of our relatives, still in the army, had suggested I go back to Iraq. This was before the presidential election, and there was some debate on the future of the war, McCain versus Obama. He had reasoned that if a Democrat won the election, I'd be there during the retreat, er, withdrawal, maybe even less than a year.

My father made a career of the military. He was in Vietnam, experienced the Tet Offensive, and would go on to retire a lieutenant colonel in the army. I was nervous as to how he would react when I told him that I didn't want to go back to Iraq.

"Don't listen to him," he said immediately. "I don't think you should go back. I've seen plenty of elections in my life, and right now, the Democrats are just talking about drawing down to get votes. You'd be a fool to believe that we're going to pull out of Iraq anytime soon."

When my father got up from the table to go to the restroom, it was just my mother and I. "I'll support whatever decision you make," she said. She then looked around the restaurant for a second before saying, "The other night, when you called with the news, your father couldn't sleep. He stayed up all night."

As of right now, though "the American combat mission

in Iraq has ended" we're still in Iraq, there is no real end in sight, and I wonder if anything will ever change. Perhaps one day I'll have a similar conversation with my own son.

I read somewhere that during the height of "The Good War," Kerouac managed to get an honorable discharge by convincing military doctors that he had "strong schizoid trends" and was thus "unfit to serve." Online you can find the official U.S. Naval Reserve file. "Facts" are as follows:

> Military: Very poor adjustment. "I just can't stand it; I like to be by myself." Sexual: He had a sex contact at age of 14 with a 32 year old woman, which upset him somewhat. Habits: Smokes pack and a half a day. Spree drinker. . . . A review of this patient's health records reveals that at recruit examination he was recognized as sufficiently abnormal to warrant duty status, and that during this period neuropsychiatric rambling, grandiose, philosophical manner . . . without any particular training or background, this patient, just prior to enlistment, enthusiastically embarked upon writing novels. He sees nothing unusual in this activity. . . . At a staff conference on June 2, 1943, the diagnosis was changed to constitutional Psychopathic State, Schizoid Personality, it being unanimously agreed that this patient has shown strong schizoid trends which have bordered upon but not yet reached the level of psychosis, but will render him unfit for service. His discharge from service is recommended.

When I reported back to Fort Benning, Georgia, I found myself numb, staring blankly out onto the historic military post from the top floor of the barracks. It's a beautiful base, surrounded by well-rooted trees, classic southern-style homes reserved for officers, a river nearby, not far from the Alabama border. The sun was about to set as soldiers, some in uniform, others not, casually walked by below. Evidence, to me, that with or without you, the army keeps rolling along.

The army changed its mind about rehiring me, kindly providing me with a one-way ticket back home once I showed them the letter the VA Medical Center in San Francisco had given me:

> Mr. Buzzell came into the evaluation visibly distressed, uncomfortable, presenting with flattened affect and speaking with soft, mumbled speech. When asked about his experiences in Iraq, he became more agitated and asked if it was necessary for him to talk about them. When told that he could refer to them very generally, he replied that one of the main incidents involved a firefight that lasted all day that took place when he was driving along a major street and his vehicle was ambushed. During the course of talking about this incident, Mr. Buzzell's speech became increasingly softer, more incoherent and more disjointed, as he was visibly disturbed and easily stimulated to flooding by this retelling. Mr. Buzzell added that there were other traumatic incidents that

occurred aside from this roadside ambush, but
in the interest of containing this vet, I told him
that the information he provided was sufficient
for the time being.

Mr. Buzzell reported that he has tried very
hard to "push out of his head" the aforemen-
tioned incident and many others since returning from Iraq. He reported that he drinks
heavily every day as a way to avoid these traumatic memories, usually to the point of black-
ing out so he can eventually fall asleep. He has
been using alcohol for the past three years as a
way to numb intrusive thoughts and remind-
ers of his combat trauma since his return from
Iraq. . . . He is severely isolated, spending most
of his day in his room and sometimes going for
several days to weeks without speaking to
anyone. Upon returning from Iraq, Mr. Buzzell
and his wife divorced. . . . When asked whether
he has thoughts of harming or killing himself,
Mr. Buzzell endorsed having a passive suicidal
ideation. . . . Mr. Buzzell also stated that he
does not own a firearm because he is scared of
what he might do with it when he is drunk . . .
while he has gotten into a couple of fistfights
in bars, he has never had an urge to hurt or kill
someone. . . . In sum, Mr. Buzzell reports extremely significant functional impairments
resulting from PTSD symptoms related to his
military service in Iraq, including severe intrusive thoughts of his trauma in Iraq, irrita-
bility, hypervigilance, difficulty sleeping,
feelings of depression, and avoidance of people,

places, and things that trigger him or remind
him of his service in Iraq.

I had recently flipped through some photos of me in
Iraq, about six or so years old now. I look so young in these
snapshots, and what is amazing is how many of them depict
me naturally smiling. Nobody back then told me to smile
when they took a snapshot.

.

A couple hours later on U.S. 50 I hit Eureka, "The Friend-
liest Town on the Loneliest Road in America." I pulled
into the gas station, filled her up again, took a piss, and
purchased coffee and a hot dog. I walked around a little to
stretch my legs. U.S. 50 goes right through the middle of
town. Every streetlight pole along this main street held a
banner bearing a service member's name; the young men
and women of Eureka, population 1,628. I felt touched by
that.

I sat down on a park bench and, sipping my coffee, wondered whether I had done the right thing while I was in
Georgia. A car passed by.

That letter I had received calling me back up to active
duty was for a deployment to Iraq, at a time when word was
going around that we were going to pull out of Iraq and
end the war. If that was the case, why in the hell did they
need me? If we were going to withdraw anyway, what's the
point?

Afghanistan, however . . . that's a whole other story. If
that letter I received had requested my presence for Operation Enduring Freedom over there in Afghanistan, I think

I might have gone. Not because I believe in the mission over there any more strongly than I believe in Operation Iraqi Freedom, but because I enjoy traveling, especially when it's on the government's dime. I've never been there before, and who knows, it could be kind of interesting. That, and the last time my life made any sense at all was when I was in the military. It didn't feel that way at the time, but it does now.

But since my orders were for Iraq, I handed the army my medical records and psychiatric evaluation. Leaving the main gate at Fort Benning that very last time, knowing I'd never have to return, I felt as though I'd just woken up from one of those dreams that don't make any sense, plaguing you the bulk of the day.

.

The entire time I was in Iraq, I wished I was stateside. Now that I'm here, there's this part of me wishing I was back there. I wonder if I wouldn't miss home as much the second time around, or even at all. You come home and think everything's going to be great, but it's not. You realize that even though after a bad day there, nothing in the world could be remotely comparable, it still seems that, just like when you were over there, every time you tell yourself things cannot possibly get any worse, they do. Tenfold.

Over the years, I've had moments I wish I had been killed in Iraq. I have a son now; I tell myself I shouldn't be having these thoughts. After tossing my coffee cup in a trash can and field-stripping my cigarette butt, I get up and make my way back to the car to hit the road again.

.

You sometimes witness strange things out in the middle of nowhere, such as the tinted-window late-model Ferrari passing by, probably on its way to Los Angeles, and then a couple of psychotic cross-country cyclists. You lose track of how long you've been driving, and suddenly the road comes to an end. I thought to myself that I'd really miss the Loneliest Road in America. It had been just me, my car, the road, my thoughts, my war, and the barren earth around me. I let my imagination go with that for a while, until far up on the horizon I see it, coming directly at me, twelve o'clock.

It was one of those compact Smart cars. It takes a certain type of individual to be able to drive around town with the word *Smart* on the back of his car. It was heading in the opposite direction, west, probably on its way to San Francisco.

Though it probably would have pleased my publisher if I went all green and did this road trip in some fuel-efficient corn-oil vehicle, the thought makes me cringe. Nothing against fuel-efficient vehicles, or the people who can afford to drive them; I'm all for the movement, but it's just not me. Not right now, that is. I'm way too vain for that. The first image that came to mind when preparing for this journey was driving an old vintage car, something sexy, like my Caliente. Just me and my car, on the road. That's it: no corporate sponsorships, no hours and hours beforehand of writing grant proposals and please-give-me-money-so-I-can-endorse-your-products-on-my-car letters, no vinyl stickers with my dot-com address plastered to the side of my vehicle to ensure people can follow me on my constantly updated blog or Twitter feed; there will

be no goddamn tweeting. Just me, my car, endless cigarettes, low-grade coffee, high-grade fuel, the road.

After the Smart car passed by, I'd let my mind wander
again when suddenly a bird shot out of nowhere right in
front of my car, resulting in a loud *thump* on my grill, an
explosion of feathers. My luck, it was probably an endan-
gered species of some sort, the first miniature flamingo
ever to be seen in Nevada, I am positive. With help from
the wind, it removed itself, blowing up only to hit my
windshield, looking at me, quickly flying off; I watched in
my rearview mirror as it hit the asphalt behind me. It flut-
tered around a bit, then stopped, dead. The small, defeated
body gradually became smaller and smaller as I continued
driving.

CHAPTER FOUR

A Veteran in a Foreign War

"If you've seen one redwood tree, you've seen them all."

RONALD REAGAN

Utah. Mormons and polygamy. Sundance and skiing.

Pulling off the freeway in downtown Salt Lake City, I cruised up to a red light and waited. The coffee shop to my left seemed packed, outdoor seating, many of the patrons covered in tattoos, coffee and cigarettes in hand. The car next to me was a Toyota, tricked out with a custom green paint job. The guy driving it couldn't have been much younger than me, and was wearing a baseball hat, cocked to the side, rap music blasting from his sound system. A scruffy hipster with a beard and bike messenger bag, though I doubt he was a bike messenger, pulled up alongside my rumbling vehicle on his fixed-gear bike. I shifted my attention over and stared at him. When the light finally turned green, he started pedaling. I put some pressure on the gas.

The first thing I noticed about my friend Pete's house when I walked in was that a woman was living there. The furniture had been moved around a bit, and the place was tidy and clean. Nothing like the way I remembered it five years before, the last time I came to visit. Back then, his place was beautifully thrashed, like a bohemian crash pad Ginsberg might have used as a backdrop to a photo shoot.

Pete's now married, which probably explains damn well the interior makeover, and the homemade meatloaf dinner his wife Kendra made. After dinner, Pete and his wife charmingly washed dishes together, as I sat at the table drinking a bottle of beer. After finishing a six-pack I felt bloated and wondered why I wasn't drunk yet.

Out for a tour of SLC with Pete, I felt a lightbulb going off in my head as we passed by the Department of Labor. We pulled into a 7-Eleven first, to grab a couple Big Gulps, and walked over to the DOL. A minivan from a local news station was parked outside. When we entered, a news camera crew was inside interviewing a lady about her job search.

I asked the girl behind the counter where the job board was located and she told me that all the jobs are now listed online, and if I wanted to find one, I only needed to sign in, and I'd be allowed to use one of their computers. There were dozens of people in front of these computers, looking for work. We signed in, took our Big Gulps with us and took a seat at the computer next to the lady who was being interviewed. Eavesdropping, we found that she was a journalism major who was now looking for something called a job.

Resisting the temptation to tap her on the shoulder and suggest she start a blog, perhaps with some affiliate links, I pulled up a Web site for a temp labor company whose slogan was "Work today, get paid today."

Sounds good. Real good, actually; and I was feeling something tingly but wasn't quite sure why that was, yet. My instincts were telling me that it was destiny. Only one way for me to find out, and that was to act on this hunch.

Excited, I wrote down the address and contact information, and we quickly drove down to where the company was located. The place was completely empty. I told the lady in sweats behind the desk that I was ready to work and could start today. She told me she was sorry, but that they didn't have any work. "Haven't for some time," she said. For the last five or six months now, every day at five in the morning they had about sixty people show up for work, and on average, they only had about ten jobs available.

I explained to her that I was interested in traveling across the country and working different jobs along the way, asking which cities she recommended. She looked up some information on her computer and told me that my best bet to find work through their agency would be to head north to Billings, Montana, or maybe Cheyenne, Wyoming. "Cheyenne has plenty of work." Casper, Wyoming; Fargo, North Dakota; and Denver, Colorado, also had work. But no matter what, don't go to the Midwest or the South—especially the South; there were absolutely no jobs there whatsoever. She had relatives who lived in the South who were in the process of leaving on account of the situation.

I jotted all this down and thanked her.

·

A few days passed, and while I planned my departure, I received a call from an 801 area code. Turned out to be in regard to a job post I had responded to on Craigslist with my laptop while drinking at a bar that had free Wi-Fi. Good things happen to those who seek them out. We had seen a bar earlier advertising free Wi-Fi, so pulled in and parked. There, after ordering a couple pints, I logged on to my computer and began scanning Web sites for possible employment opportunities. I've always been curious as to why bars offer free Wi-Fi, and now I knew. They offer it so that you can look for a job while unemployed.

The lady on the phone asked if I was still interested in the position. Containing my excitement to the best of my ability, I told her yes, I was.

Pete gave me a ride to the interview, explaining on the way that it's a lower-middle-class part of town. He went on to explain that he doesn't really go there much, since it's kind of "ghetto." While he waited in his car in a nearby church parking lot, listening to Michael Savage on his car stereo, I walked up to the house and knocked on the door. I immediately heard the stomp of little feet running around like there was some kind of day care going on inside. Then the door to opportunity opened up to me, and a kindly housewife welcomed me inside. The smell of stew was in the air, and I saw at least three kids—all running around—as I made my way, as directed, to the table in the middle of the room and took a seat. The lady who owned and operated the business sat across from me with a bunch of miscellaneous folders and paperwork organized into neat stacks set in front of her. To my left, a few steps away from me was the kitchen where a lady, slightly older, stood stirring a pot on the stove, which I suspected was the source of stew I had smelled when I'd first walked in. She asked for my name, and when I gave it, the lady cooking quickly turned around, making it possible for me to view her stellar sweatshirt, which had deer embroidered onto it. With a subtle red-state accent, she asked if I was the guy on the phone who was traveling across the country. I told her I was, and she immediately got excited telling me how cool that was. "You know what that reminded me of? What's the name of that one guy? You know, that one book where those two guys go hitchhiking across the country? Hmm, what's the name of that . . ."

I was amazed that this lady knew of it.

"*On the Road?*"

"Yes! That one! It reminded me of that!"

The interview consisted of only a few questions: how was my driving record, when could I start, and how much or often could I work. I was perplexed that nothing was said about a background check; there was no request to see my birth certificate, nor was I asked to provide my social security number. She explained to me that I would be contracted out, and I would get to use their van lease-free, as long as I returned it at the end of the day with the same amount of gas in it as when I left. They would provide all the ice cream, and I keep 30 percent of each sale. I should have paid more attention in math class back in school; at $1 to $1.50 an ice cream bar, how many ice cream bars would I have to sell during a full nine-hour shift to make it worth my time? Confused, I don't ask her how much an average day would rake in, nor whether there was a 401(k) plan involved. She told me that weekends were always good, especially when it's sunny and hot like it had been the past several weeks. After the interview, I walked slowly back to the church parking lot where Pete was waiting, a block away, and got into the car, bummed. Pete asked me what happened and, more importantly, if I had gotten the job.

I smiled.

·

The next morning when I woke up, it was as if God was telling me not to get a job. I step outside with a cup of coffee and a cigarette, and what should it do on my first day as an ice cream truck driver in Salt Lake City, Utah? Rain. It wasn't a light rain, it was downright pouring. How the fuck did that happen? It had been sunny and hot the entire time I'd been there, and I didn't know what to do. Is it like a game that gets canceled due to rain? Do I show up to work today? It could be a waste of time for all parties involved to try and sell ice cream on a rainy day, plus I was a bit hung over from going out to the bar last night to celebrate my new employment. I called the lady up to see if she still needed me to come into work, and she said, "Absolutely! Get down here! Some of our best days have been on days where it's rained!"

I had gone online the night before to do some research on the profession. I was curious to find out how much ice cream trucks made, how many units I could hope to push on the good children of SLC, so I Googled "ice cream truck," checking out various recent articles; I was shocked to see that there were dozens. As I read, I seriously wondered how many ice cream truck drivers get killed each year in the line of duty. The statistics must be staggering.

There had to be a monument for them somewhere, because these articles were brutal. "Ice Cream Truck Driver Says Arson Was Attempted Murder," "Three Charged with Hate Crime in Ice Cream Truck Attack," "Two Marin County Men Face Charges in What Police Say Was an Attempted Highway Heist of an Ice Cream Truck," "Mister Softee Driver Busted for Stopping Ice Cream Truck to Buy Drugs." All recent.

Pete waited again in his car down the street as I went to sign in and pick up the truck. When I showed up at the house, one of the kids I had seen the day before was seated at the dinner table playing a game of blocks with two packs of cigarettes while Grandma took me out to the ice cream truck to show me how it works. She went over the entire inventory and told me which ice creams sell, which don't, how to drive the vehicle, operate the Slow Children sign, and turn on the sound system, which has a couple dozen ice cream chimes to choose from. After that, I was all ready to enter the world of the employed again. She gave me directions to a town called Magna and suggested I start there and make my way back: "Yes, it's a poor neighborhood, but you'll make a killing there. For some reason kids there love ice cream."

She helped back the ice cream truck out of their garage, waving me off. I drove over to pick Pete up in front of a house down the block with gang graffiti spray-painted on the outside. After I picked him up, the rain cleared up, and the sun was starting to come out. We were locked and loaded on our way to Magna. Pete's wife called, wished us luck. "Try not to get shot," she said.

I was starting to wonder what in the hell we were doing wrong when all of a sudden at 11:15 a.m. a girl popped out of a building to our vehicle's ten o'clock, guided by her mother. The two of them walked over, and I asked the little girl what she wanted. She told me she wanted a Rainbow Pop. Easy enough; we had two grown males in charge.

I looked, but didn't see any Rainbow Pops, so asked her to pick something else. She frowned and pointed at a sticker on the side of the truck. I leaned out the ice cream truck window to see what she was pointing at, and dove into the back of the truck on the hunt for a Fudgsicle.

A few moments later I poked my head back outside the truck to tell her that we didn't have that either and asked her to again pick something else. The frown on the little girl's face turned to borderline anger. I couldn't tell if she wanted to kick me or start crying, she could go either way, so I grabbed a King Cone, thanked her for her patience, and told her that it was free. Her mother asked, "Did you guys just steal the truck?"

I didn't know how to answer. Just then Pete, who like me was breaking a sweat, exclaimed, "I found it!"

We made our sale, and after that we both needed a drink. So we parked the truck outside the neighborhood VFW bar and walked in. An old dusty American flag hung above the bar, and about a half dozen day drinkers were silently inside looming at the bar. One guy, sitting at a table in the corner, had his head down, sleeping, while *The Gilmore Girls* played on the television. After ordering a pint, I got to talking with one of the old-timers, telling him how much of a pain in the ass it was trying to sell ice cream. He told me to follow him after we were done with the beer, and that he'd drive us over to a trailer park community that always has dozens of kids running around. After we polished off our beers, we did as he asked, following his white pickup truck to the Promised Land, the trailer park community. We didn't sell shit.

As I drove the truck through other residential neighborhoods in search of little kids, I wondered if this is what a child molester on the hunt might also find himself doing. We came across several other ice cream trucks also driving through our area of operation, one of which we tailed for a bit, and another I pulled up alongside to ask, "Hey how much do you make?" He didn't seem to speak English, and I had no idea what in the world he was saying; I'm not even really sure he understood the question. It made me wonder if this was his first job here in America.

The only rush we had that day was a Mexican family who came over once we pulled into a small park. Afterward we drove around another neighborhood, several houses again covered in gang graffiti. Pete and I felt bad for not selling any ice cream, and we felt even worse for having eaten some of the profits when we got hungry. Our last sale of the day went to a little black girl who pushed her wheelchair to the curb and sat there patiently waiting for us to pull up. She was wearing a T-shirt with the American flag on it. She only had a dollar in loose change on her, and she asked, "Can I have that one, please?" as she pointed to an ice cream bar that cost $1.50. I really did not want to take her money, and I felt bad doing so, but I sold her the ice cream bar for her dollar. She said thank you, and we called it a day.

●

At the gas station I estimated that for a full nine hours of driving around way below the legal residential speed limit, about fifteen miles per hour, the amount I would have to put into the vehicle would be $7. That didn't move the gas gauge one bit. So I put $5 more in. It barely moved. I put another $7 in low-octane fuel in, and it moved the meter a bit closer to where I needed it to be. Fuck it. Close enough. The amount that I spent on gas that day was $19.

When I checked the truck back in, I sat around and chatted with the grandma while her daughter went through all the ice cream in the truck to see how much we had sold. We talked about where I'd been so far, and where I was thinking about heading. She gave me some advice on places I should check out along the way, like the town in Montana where the Unabomber lived. When her daughter came back inside the house, she pulled up an Excel spreadsheet on her computer and started listing off what I had sold, handing me cash. I assumed I would be scheduled to work the following day since I had agreed to work the entire weekend, but she told me that wasn't necessary and wished me luck on my travels. I thanked them all and left.

The amount that I made, on 30 percent commission, for a full nine hours of work was a whopping $10.50. Since I had paid $19 for gas, what I really made was a negative $8.50. I wondered how the other ice cream truck drivers made a living.

At the end of the workday I was mentally, physically, and psychologically exhausted. Back at the house, Pete's wife had a steak dinner prepared for us. We stopped by the liquor store to pick up a couple bottles of wine with the money we had made that day, all negative $8.50 of it. We picked up four bottles of their cheapest. The four bottles of wine put us at a negative $36.

The steak was delicious.

CHAPTER FIVE

Changing Atmospheric Conditions

"Travel is only glamorous in retrospect."

PAUL THEROUX

Shortly after crossing the Utah-Wyoming state border, I pulled off the freeway. I hung out a few hours, wandering aimlessly. I got back onto the freeway, then off again. Hung out. Back onto the freeway, off again. Gas station, diner, a motel or two, a couple chain fast food joints, maybe a Walmart, and residential houses with locked front doors, their inhabitants suspiciously closing their blinds as you walk past. That's it. Then back onto the freeway, drive for a bit. Repeat. This went on and on, each time feeling more uncomfortable than the last.

It then hit me: I was totally fucked. This path that I was now on scared the hell out of me. It was just me and I-80, but I feared this might be the climax of my trip. I felt like I was stuck in some unreasonably long, drawn-out indie film, no plot whatsoever, and nobody could find the remote to change the channel. I was the main character, stuck living in this film.

So far the rising action, leading up to this potential

climax, had been quite dull. That's my conflict. *Nickel-and-Dimed in Salt Lake City?* Let's see, since then, I'd played a game of bingo at a VFW hall, driven a lot, and witnessed the groundbreaking of a new library in Lyman, Wyoming, "A Great Place to Grow." Three feet of gas station hot dog and dozens of energy drink containers later, I stopped in for some shitty Chinese. My fortune cookie read:

> One of the first things you should look for in a problem is its positive side.

I angrily left no tip. Basically, what I needed to figure out was a way for me to hurry the fuck up and get to the climax, wherever and whatever the hell that is, then hurry up and get to the *falling* action part, "during which the tension is palpably eased; and then finally *the resolution*, or ending."

You have to keep all this in mind while driving across the country working on a book for a big-name publisher out in New York City with in-house lawyers who would love to do their job and come after you for that book advance money that they kindly gave you in good faith . . . which you've now pretty much blown on booze. The thought of all this was making me want to drink, a lot. It also made me want to disappear, permanently. All this to say I felt like a man on the run, which maybe I'd pretend was the case, for now.

I was noticing a new sound coming from my engine, much like air being funneled through a plastic straw. I tried to not think too hard about that as I made my way to Green River, Wyoming.

•

Slowly rolling into the gravel parking lot of a motel, I noticed that all the other vehicles were pickups, nearly all with blue-and-white Michigan plates.

The lady working the front desk looked straight out of a David Lynch movie. I requested to stay one night, and she told me that most of the folks who stayed there do so for a lot longer, a week, several weeks, sometimes months. She mentioned she had several who had been living there for nearly six months: "They come here from out of state to work." With my wheels now spinning, I thanked her for the information. Dropping my shit off in my room, I made my way over to the bar I'd noticed by the train depot.

Discovering that I was a war veteran, a guy my age wearing a cowboy hat, Wranglers, and a huge belt buckle the size of a dinner plate kindly introduced himself as a "redneck from the sticks," and thanked me for my service. He bought me a beer and started, "I don't want to offend you, or anything like that, but can I ask you a question?" He hemmed and hawed, and given past experience, I thought I knew exactly what he was going to ask. *Why in the world did you join the military?* Shortly followed by his personal opinions on the war, all along the lines of how we should have never invaded Iraq, the war was wrong, I support the troops but not the war, etc. Especially by those who say, "Well, I'm glad you're back," which is always said with a subtle implication of being against the war, as if the gas-powered vehicles that they're driving all have a "Bring the troops home now!" bumper sticker placed on the back of them, which they're not telling you about. I've heard it all a million times over. Instead, the complete opposite happened. He asked me, "Why'd you come back?"

I just stared at him blankly, not knowing how to answer that one.

"I'm serious, why'd you come back?"

While I struggled to think how to answer, an intoxicated female stumbled over, eyeballing his cowboy hat. She took his hat off, exposing his bald head, and jovially told him that she liked his hat, a lot, and wanted to wear it. Irritated by the interruption, he politely agreed, getting up from his bar stool, telling me he'd be right back. A couple minutes later, he returned, wearing a mesh camouflage hunting cap, and picked up where we left off.

He explained to me that there are no jobs anymore in this country, and at least over there, I had the opportunity to make some pretty good money. He said he had looked into driving a truck in Iraq, and had been serious about it, but at the last minute he chose not to, as he felt it'd be too dangerous. He said he didn't want to go over there unless he could bring his firearm with him; as a contractor, he could not do so legally.

"The Armed Forces provide firearms," I told him. I caught him off-guard when I asked why he hadn't simply enlisted in the military. I told him I was sure he could have driven a truck for them, no problem. It was as though that thought had never occurred to him. He stuttered, dumbfounded, unable to explain why he hadn't joined up.

After a few more beers, he changed the topic by asking whether or not I knew what a jackalope was. When I told him that I didn't know this creature, forgetting for a minute that I'm not at home, I expected him to pull out his iPhone and update his Facebook status with something like, "At a bar next to another dumb Californian who doesn't know what a jackalope is. LMFAO." Instead, he kindly informed me that jackalopes are the result of bored antelopes. "They fuck jackrabbits." Since I told him that I was driving through Wyoming on I-80, he asked me whether I had seen the wooden things on the side of the freeway on my way into town. I told him I had, and that I had wondered what they were. He told me that they're there to break up the wind during snow season. "People from the West Coast and East Coast are stupid," he told me, which is what some people from both coasts think of Middle Americans. For fear of being escorted out, I keep my mouth shut on that one. He goes on, "When they come here, if you tell them that those things are bleachers to watch the jackalopes, they'll believe it! They're stupid. People here, they remember your name. You watch the news, no one gives a fuck about Montana, Idaho, Wyoming. You only hear about those states when they get to the weather report, that's it. 'Oh, it was windy today in Wyoming.' "

With my car windows fully rolled down, I felt a liberating breeze as I left Green River. By the time I got to Cheyenne, Wyoming, I was just as lost as when I began.

CHAPTER SIX

Down and Out in Cheyenne

*"Hard times arouse an instinctive desire for
authenticity."*

COCO CHANEL

One of those bronze plaques greeted me by the main entrance, declaring that the building was a registered historic
landmark. Behind the concierge desk hung an oil painting
of a Native American. He looked proud as I walked across
the marble lobby floor, toward the front desk, passing a
well-dressed couple rolling their airport luggage along. I
was quickly getting the impression that I was walking into
Cheyenne's version of the Waldorf-Astoria, which made
me want to step into character, adapt to my surroundings.
Head up, as if I'd just left my keys with the valet, I radiated importance; the spotlight was on me. I belonged here,
I possessed a confidence others envy. No one here needed
to know I'm just some unemployed drifter, with a limited
vocabulary, driving across America in an old, beat-up car
in search of a plot.

I figured a nice hotel in a small town ought to be as
much as a mid- to low-range hotel in a big city; that was
my logic, anyway. I approached the front desk, where I

asked the lady on the other side—well dressed, hair pulled back—how much it'd cost me for a night in their swanky establishment. She told me it'd be $120 for the night. I immediately forgot I was in character and asked for a discounted rate. She apologized, telling me that wouldn't be possible. I gasped, and quickly told her thank you. I debated for a second whether or not I should inquire as to where the closest Barneys New York is located, but decided not to be an asshole. As I headed toward the door, setting my sights on the Motel 8 I'd noticed getting off the freeway, she quickly pitched me on the surrounding location and its several restaurants, one of which apparently served the best steaks in all of Wyoming. She told me that this hotel was located in historic downtown Cheyenne, which didn't impress me at all—so far, all historic meant was a bunch of old buildings with For Lease signs posted on them. My eyes remained at half-mast. Working hard now, she quickly typed some stuff into her computer, telling me that they did have some rooms available that evening, and if I wanted to, I could have one at a discounted rate of only $70. I debated this for a minute. Seventy dollars a night is still way over budget, but my logic kicked in, and I rationalized that it might be the equivalent of a $700-a-night hotel in New York City.

All along I-80 the going rate at a seedy roadside motel had seemed to be in the vicinity of $35–$45, plus tax. It would be nice to pay not that much more for a night where I didn't have to wake up itching with bedbug bites, or worry about bedsheets with old cum stains. It would be nice to have a warm shower that worked. I didn't want to be impulsive, so I told her thanks, but I'd think about it while I took a walk around the neighborhood, see what else was here. If I decided to stay, I'd be back in a bit.

•

Head down, I made my way back to the parking garage, wondering what I should do next. Should I stick around, or keep on driving? A block away, I come across a doormat advertising a hotel.

I stop and look up, seeing one of those red, white, and blue "Support Local Business" stickers by the door handle; it looks like somebody has attempted to peel it off, failing. Below it is another sticker stating that the building is a smoke-free environment.

There was absolutely nobody around, no foot traffic, no cars driving by or even parked on the street. The building looked vacant, deserted, like all the others I had passed. When I put my hand on the door, I was surprised that it actually opened. An old wooden staircase, lined on both sides with mirrors, led up to the hotel lobby. At the top of the stairs, I could see a mounted deer head poking out from behind the registration desk. The suspense—What could possibly lie ahead?—was killing me. I began the climb up, each step creaking, almost deafening in the silence. I looked over to my left and saw my reflection staring back from a shattered mirror. I noticed that I had put on a couple pounds since the start of this trip, at least five, and I debated whether this was healthy weight or whether I needed to go on a diet. The place had a smell somewhere in the range of an old bookstore located in a condemned building. Once I had made it to the top of the stairs, I saw a note hung below a small American flag: "Back in 15 minutes."

I could now hear a loud commotion echoing from one of the rooms down the hallway, like an out-of-control party. A voice behind me asked, "You needin' a room?" Stunned, though the voice had a tone of kindness, I quickly turned around to see standing before me, wearing jeans and a sleeveless shirt, a kind fellow with a mustache. He was so skinny, it looked as though walking was a true effort. I told the guy yes, I was, and he reached out his hand to shake. I gave him a firm shake, fearful I might do him harm. He guided me to the manager's room, which also had a note stuck to the door stating "Back in 15 minutes." He turned around and, looking back at me, motioned for me to follow him. "Come on down to my cell, I'll let you hang out down there till she comes back." So I followed him down the hall, over to Room 136, the source of all the noise echoing up and down the hallway. On the way, he told me that a handful of other residents were also hanging out, waiting for the manager to show up. When he opened the door to Room 136, the tiny room, the size of a janitor's office, was filled with the fog of tobacco. I said hello to everyone, five others completely wasted on Schlitz, the room littered with empty aluminum cans of similar quality. I was handed an empty to ash in, and a guy wearing a "Hooters, Fort Lauderdale" T-shirt offered me his chair in the corner. I thanked him and as I took the seat, was asked if I'd like a shot. Quickly handed a plastic bottle of cheap vodka I took a swig. As the gang began to introduce themselves, I was handed a Schlitz. I was thinking I might inquire about weekly rates.

I have a fear of other people, and I need to not project that fear when I enter a room filled with strangers, since people can pick up on it. I reminded myself to be friendly, outgoing, positive.

"Hey, how's it going? My name's Colby."

Some nodded, others said hello and stuck out their hands for a shake. I began sizing them up, speculating on their career choices. Truck drivers?

"Coleman? Nice to meet you. You want another shot?"

Sure. We passed the plastic vodka bottle around the room for another round, and I tried not to think of the possibility of contracting some nasty incurable disease transmitted via saliva. I was feeling a bit proud of myself for making the effort to turn over a new leaf, be more sociable, all those annoying qualities I somewhat dislike in others.

The bottle made four or five laps around the room, me turning it down that last trip. "Pussy!" exclaimed Hooters guy, next to me. I changed my mind and took one last shot. He cheered.

The guy with the southern accent then asked, "Where you from, brother?"

Depending upon my geographic location, answering this question could, in some situations, get me killed. I knew that, and heart skipping a beat, I decided to go ahead and tell them the truth.

"California."

I knew full well that answer wasn't going to be good enough; I could have sworn I heard one of them exclaim,

"Strike one!" They wanted specifics. The guy in the opposite corner, leaning up against the wall, barely able to stand, raised an eyebrow, heavily observing me.

As I walk through the shadow of the valley of death . . . fuck it, just tell them. No one lives forever.

"San Francisco."

The guy holding himself up in the corner released an "Ewww"; another looked equally disgusted, as though he'd discovered his beer can was in fact actually filled with piss.

"San Francisco?" Skinny asked, "Whereabouts?"

So far, I'm liking him the most. When I mentioned I lived in the Tenderloin district, I was shocked to find that a couple of them knew exactly where that was, and had lived there themselves.

One of them went on to tell a story. "I drive a truck, and one time I was there getting fucked up. I hired a couple Mexicans, and we went down there. One guy was like, take a walk with me, and I was like, goddamn, man, fuck that."

He was wasted, moving from one thought to another. "I say I'ma buy me some, how much a hundred dollar get me, buy what you want, you know? So I buy me an eight-ball for a hundred dollars, you know, and I got me fffuuuccck-kkkeeeddd uuuppp!!! This was in ninety-fucking-eight. I was in Idaho, and I bought that rig. I, um, go to the massage parlor, and then get me two hookers out of them yellow pages over there, snorted all that shit and got me laid up there in the motel for three days and flew back to Idaho and told them to fuck themselves and gave 'em the truck right there."

He then went into talking about his ex-wife. "She

got all my fucking furniture and my car, you know. She wanted half! And I want half of what's mine, right, you know, I work my ass off for all that mutha-fucking stuff. That goddamn living room set cost six fucking thousand dollars man, that shit ain't cheap. Ethan Allen mutha-fucking shit! You know, I paid six hundred fucking dollars for a damn end table! It's killing me, man, I want my mutha-fuckin' shit, man."

When I told them how I was going to head down to the day labor place the following morning to find work, they all knew exactly where that was, and a couple of them told me they were banned from there for life.

Not only were they all drinking the cheapest alcohol money could buy, but I noticed that they were all smoking the cheapest generic-brand cigarettes, too, one right after another, straight out of soft packs, lighting up with free matches. I smoke Marlboro Lights. For fear of appearing too bourgeois, I decided to keep my pack in my pocket; I didn't want to offend my new friends. Instead, I offered one of them fifty cents for a smoke. He handed me one, turning down the two quarters I offered. I thanked him and I pulled out my lighter, ashing in my empty Schlitz can.

•

Eventually I felt I was on the way to drunk, so I excused myself by saying that I was going to check to see if the manager was back. She wasn't, but her husband, Joe, was. He looked like a Joe. He wore an old sun-faded American-flag do-rag, and told me that they did have a room available—cash only—and if I wanted to take a look at it, I could.

Now that I had a room, I needed my own liquor to go with it. Joe gave me directions to a store nearby, around the corner and down the street. As I was leaving the building, I noticed that there was now a police officer looming in the very same hallway where I had just been. Instead of sticking around to find out what that was all about, I quickly exited back down the wooden stairs. Once outside, a slight buzz on, I came across a used bookstore, which had a sign on its front door advertising a sale on all Western paperbacks.

The owner of the shop welcomed me in, telling me that he had purchased the place a couple years ago. I asked if he had a copy of *On the Road*. He guided me to the literature section, telling me that he probably didn't have a copy right now, that it's really popular with high school readers—when he gets a used copy, it doesn't last too long on his shelves. The only related books he did have were a couple biographies on Kerouac, and a vintage paperback edition of *Maggie Cassidy*. Since he went through so many copies of *On the Road*, I asked him if he knew about Cheyenne's connection with the book. He wasn't aware of any folklore or anything like that, though he told me with a smile that he did remember Kerouac doesn't speak too highly of Cheyenne.

I told him I was traveling across the country and when I mentioned the hotel around the corner, he shook his head, disgusted. "I would never . . . send anyone over there."

He went on to tell me he knew exactly what everybody who stays at the hotel drank because all they did all day was walk past his bookstore, back and forth to the liquor store a block away; I made a mental note to find an alternate return route after my own walk to buy liquor.

"People die there all the time." Not too long ago, he told me, three residents passed away in one month. "People who stay there are on their way out."

Did this mean I was on my way out? I decided to go ahead and make it a bit awkward, telling him that I was actually staying there. He changed it over to a story about a sixty-something-year-old resident living there who pretty much stayed in his room all day long, a bit of a loner, but every morning, like clockwork, the guy stopped by his bookstore and left him a copy of yesterday's newspaper. If the shop owner was not there, or if the shop was closed, he'd leave the paper on the doorstep. He'd apparently been doing that for years. He told me that if Obama's face was on the front page, which was quite often, this guy would always draw glasses and a mustache on him.

They had a bunch of music downstairs, so I went down to check out their vinyl LPs. While I was flipping through them, a guy came down to ask me if I was the guy asking about Kerouac earlier.

He looked like a construction worker—mesh hat, worn blue jeans, sleeves removed from his shirt, a rolled-up newspaper sticking out of his back pocket along with a pair of construction gloves. He started off by telling me, "I'm a first-edition kind of guy myself, I like to collect me them first editions. I even got me an *On the Road* first edition." We talked about Kerouac and *On the Road* for well over an hour. Afterward, I purchase a few Steinbeck hardcovers, some of them first editions: *The Wayward Bus*, *The Moon Is Down*, and *The Winter of Our Discontent.*

I ran into the Kerouac fan again outside the bookstore, on my way over to the liquor store. As I walked away, his last words for me were, "Yep, once upon a time he was here."

•

Since there was no fridge in my room, I had picked up half a dozen bottles of cheap wine. The manager was now back. "Sorry, I was at Curves," she said. I handed her the $120, in cash, for the week-long rental. She handed me a door key, as well as a complimentary roll of toilet paper— the first one free, every roll after would cost me fifty cents. I thanked her, not bothering to ask if they had a Wi-Fi connection, wondering whether I'd even be able to find a bar in Cheyenne with this amenity. I got to my room: flat red carpet, a bit dirty, but whatever. I turned on the plastic Daewoo television set, seeing that the person who lived here before me had left it set to CNN; I left it that way and cracked open a bottle of my wine. The room came with an empty metal soup can to be used as an ashtray. I sat there in a chair Goodwill probably wouldn't even accept as a donation, smoking my cigarette. I thought about the smoke-free-environment sticker I had seen on the front door as I ashed on the carpet. Between commercials for insurance policies and something called "pajama jeans," I watched Anderson Cooper tell me how bad the economy is, and how everybody is losing their jobs. For the first time in a long while, watching television didn't make me depressed.

While finishing my second bottle of wine, feeling

updated on current events, I turned the television off and sat there on the sofa, staring at the wall. Somewhere down the hallway was a commotion, and again I felt no desire to find out what it was all about. My thoughts were consumed with this feeling that there was something missing in this room of mine. I was vexed trying to determine what it was exactly, and then it hit me. I need a dream board.

A dream board is a visual aid you set up to help you achieve whatever goals you might have, like a collage. Say your dream is to be rich, with a huge house, a fancy car, a picturesque family that never fights and is always smiling. Well, if that's not a nightmare to you, and truly is your dream, you post pictures depicting all that on your dream board, and according to my sister, who believes in this shit, if you stare at your dream board long enough—somehow, someway—it'll all miraculously happen to you.

Since I didn't have any magazines to cut and paste from as inspiration for my dream board, I decided to instead just post words related to my dreams. I pulled out my pen and notebook, and, after taking a huge swig of wine, I put the end of the pen in my mouth and gently gnaw while thinking long and hard about the words I wanted to use. I put down "Writer," but then tore that page out of my notebook, crumpled it up, and shot a three-pointer toward the wastebasket. Missed.

I needed to keep my dreams realistic. I was beginning to freak when I realized that I couldn't think of any dreams that were—my imagination was drifting to impossibilities like "Dinosaur Tamer"—so I quickly asked myself what I needed or wanted. The first thing that came to mind was a plot. A plot that would give my book—or my life—a purpose, a meaning, a point. I decided that this plot would be a good short-term goal for me, but it was too abstract. I needed to think long-term; what was a good long-term goal? A job would be a nice, obtainable long-term goal; work gives your life meaning, and since that's what I needed, I write down, "Employment."

When I couldn't think of any other words to post on my dream board, I decide to give up and be happy focused on just that one dream. I realized then that I had nothing—no tape or thumb tacks like my sister had—to post it up with on my dream board, so I improvised. I turned the sink on, got the paper soaking wet, and very satisfactorily slapped it up on the wall.

I stared at it for a while, until eventually it dried, slipping to the ground. No longer interested in my dream board, I turned the light off, and went to bed.

•

After about five or six turns of the key, I was about to say fuck it and call the toll-free USAA roadside assistance number when finally, finally, the engine fired up. I let it run for a bit, spewing toxic carbon out into the atmosphere. Once I felt the engine was running properly, all heated up, I pulled the vehicle out of the parking garage and rolled onto West Lincolnway, eastbound.

The sun was just now peeking up over the horizon. Waiting patiently for a red light at the corner of Central Avenue, I noticed that most of the enormous pickup trucks rumbling around were covered in rust, and looked like they'd been buried underground for the last decade or two.

It was impressive that they still ran. Occasionally I'd see a brand-new F-150 or F-250 with massive engine and tires, big silver industrial steel toolbox bolted into the bed, full of heavy and expensive tools. We were all heading in the same direction, all on our way to work. Maybe a couple of them were on their way to *finding* work, as I was, but looking at these men—the rugged men who drive these pickup trucks, staring silently at the road ahead, bright and early in the morning, sipping shitty gas station coffee while puffing away on cheap generic soft-pack cigarettes, old sun-faded ball caps emblazoned "Makita," thick salty sweat rings all along the brim, bent down to shield their eyes and face from the sun—I didn't think the majority were looking for work. No, these men had work, and had done real work their entire lives.

When the light finally turned green, one by one we headed down the same path, together.

I parked the Caliente over in a residential neighborhood, in front of a one-story with a chain-link fence around it two blocks from where I had to be that morning. I locked her up, and as I began to walk away, I noticed steam coming from under her hood. Since it was a bit cold, my first thought was that it's just morning moisture coming up off my engine. But when I lifted the hood, I saw that there was green shit splattered all over the engine, dripping down my radiator.

Was this God once again telling me not to get a job? I'll worry about all this later, I thought; first I've got to get a goddamn job.

On the street corner directly across from the day labor

place I'd been referred to in Utah was a tire repair shop. I saw an auto mechanic, wearing greasy blue work khakis, in front of the shop rolling a tire with his hands, a lit cigarette hanging from his lips. Since I was running a couple minutes early, I stopped to talk with him about my problem. He told me that they didn't do radiators, just tires; they usually sent radiator work over to another guy clear on the other side of town. That didn't help me any, and when I asked him if there were any radiator guys at all in the neighborhood, or within walking distance, he told me no, there weren't. I thanked him and proceeded to ignore my car problems, making my way to the day labor agency to pick up some freelance work, Cheyenne Edition.

.

About a dozen people were standing around, sullenly smoking, outside. I made my way past them, walking inside with my game face on, eager to work, radiating positive energy. The lobby inside was like the waiting room to poverty; a couple dozen white plastic chairs set up, nearly all the seats taken. Most occupants looked like they had already been waiting around a couple hours, it now only being seven o'clock.

The television up in the corner was playing some work safety information video. When I told the guy behind the counter wearing a blue polo shirt and glasses that I was looking for work, I could see written on the job board behind him that they had a job available for an auto mechanic with three years' experience and his own tools. I was tempted to ask them if they could add next to that, "Mechanic who can fix a radiator on a 1964 Mercury

Comet Caliente desperately needed. Will trade beer and NAME BRAND cigarettes for time and labor. See Colby."

After a couple questions, including if I've ever worked for them and "Do you have two forms of ID?" the guy behind the counter sat me down at a folding table in the back, which had one of those keypads you see at the check-out aisle at the grocery store that you type your debit card information into, and a binder containing test questions for me to answer to the best of my ability to determine whether I was employable.

With the guy standing next to me to help get me going, I sat down in the chair. The first couple questions that he guided me through were pretty basic, along the lines of whether I was male or female, and whether I knew my social security number. When the *What race are you?* question came up, he told me to mark one if I was white, two if I was black, and three if I was Hispanic. That's it.

He stood there for a couple seconds with his hands on his hips and a patient smile on his face, waiting for me to punch the correct number into the machine. I just kind of sit there for a couple seconds, looking at him, waiting for more options. Finally I ask, "What about Asian?" His smile dissipated into a look of confusion. I could see the wheels turning in his head as he thought about it. He told me that he did not know what to press for Asian, and asked me to wait as he went back to the front desk to check the manual.

I'm half white and half Asian. I remember that when I was in D.C. for the inauguration, I saw many wearing T-shirts that read, "My President Is Black." So I think people who are half white go with whatever other half they are, like the president. I hadn't seen any fellow Asian-Americans waiting around for a job—come to think of it, the only Asians I'd seen so far here in Cheyenne all worked at the Chinese buffet near my hotel—so I thought it might be best to tell them that I was Asian, in case they were hip to the whole diversity thing. It might help me land more jobs here.

While I was waiting for him to find out what an Asian is to do, a Native American at the table behind me, his long hair tied back in a ponytail, was doing paperwork, organizing time cards. "Hey," he said in a low voice, one I hadn't heard since high school, like he was helping me cheat. "On that test, whatever you do, do not say that you've ever beaten somebody up on the job, stolen anything from an employer, or done any drugs. Even if you have, just say no to those questions." I thanked him for his help just as the guy came back, a smile back on his face, and told me to go ahead and press four for Asian.

There were about seventy-five multiple-choice questions, clustered in groups revolving around four basic concepts:

Had I ever knocked somebody out while on a job?

Had I ever stolen work or office supplies?

Had I ever cheated on my taxes or received government assistance?

Was I a drug addict or alcoholic?

For example, question 34 asked, "When do you drink alcohol?" a reasonable multiple-choice option being "While driving." I noticed that for a lot of the drug- and alcohol-related questions where they asked whether you partook, the multiple-choice option never included "No." All they had available was "Seldom or Never."

When I was all done with the test, I went up to the front counter. The guy with the glasses was busy sending a couple of people out on a job, so a very kind petite lady assisted me by sending my test answers electronically up the chain, the test results instantly indicating that I had passed. According to them, I was employable.

I was handed some forms to fill out. One asked about prior work experience, whether I had experience welding, pouring concrete, and the like. I marked down that I had experience in pretty much everything, which is somewhat true. A lot of these things that they were asking about— janitorial work, gardening, manual labor—were things that I got experience doing while I was in the military. If they sent me out on a job that I didn't have any prior experience with, I was pretty sure I could figure it out. When I joined the army, one of the very first things they handed me at basic training was not a weapon but a lovely mop and bucket to wipe down the barracks bay. I was a mop prodigy; I figured it out pretty quick. I reasoned that I could do the same thing here. When I got down to some of the questions specific to armed forces work experience, one of the questions was, "Is this person deceased? If so, enter date of death." It seemed this agency had experience placing dead people, taking the notion of equal opportunity to a somewhat new level.

After more paperwork, W-2s and crap like that, the lady asked me whether I wanted to take a drug test, which is optional. She explained that I would be available for more jobs if I was drug-free; some employers like that. Trying really hard to remember the last time I did any drugs, while at the same time trying really hard not to look like I was trying really hard to remember the last time I'd done any drugs, I tell her, Sure, I'll take the test. She handed me a plastic cup to piss in, which I brought to the bathroom. When done, I returned it to her, setting it on the counter. She looked at the label on the side of the plastic cup and said, "Oh, good. You passed."

I was caught off guard by this. "What?!" I exclaimed without thinking. "I passed?"

"Yeah. You passed." She studied me. "Why are you so surprised?" she asked.

"Umm . . ." I then explained that it wasn't the results that surprised me. "I've never done any drugs before, ever. I don't like the way they make me feel." I tell her that what I am surprised about is how fast the test results came back in; for some reason, I thought it would take a couple days or weeks for that to happen, that they would actually have to test my piss to get a result. She chuckled a bit and explained to me that the side of the cup had a sticker that instantly gave the results.

Now that I'd passed all these tests with flying colors and was available to work that day, she made me sign my name on the work clipboard on the counter along with all the other people looking for work. She told me they would call me if they had any work today. If not, I should show up the following morning at five. I would check in just like I did now, and if any work came in that they believed I was

qualified to do, they'd send me out. If not, I'd get the opportunity to sit around all day waiting for work, just like
everybody else here.

I felt really good—excited even—about my future. I'd
passed all the tests that they threw at me, including the
safety test I winged. When I stepped outside, I threw my
sunglasses on, lit up a smoke, and thought to myself that
this must be how it feels to get a high score on the SAT.
Then I remembered the damn car, and started wondering
what the fuck I was going to do with that. Then I saw it:
right there in front of me, only one block away from where
that guy at the tire shop had told me there were absolutely
no auto mechanics in this area, was an auto shop. Buck's
Auto Repair.

•

A guy who appeared to be my age, sleeves rolled up, was
working on a mid-1960s Chevy Camaro in the garage when
I walked up. We shook hands and I told him all about my
problem, and that she was parked right around the corner.
He told me to go ahead and drive it in, he'd take a look
and tell me what's wrong. So I did, and when I drove it up,
he saw the vintage black and yellow California plates and
asked whether I was from there. I told him I was, and of
course the next question was, What the hell are you doing
here in Cheyenne? I told him I was driving across the
country looking for work, and I heard I could find it here.
He nodded as he lifted the hood, knowing exactly what I
was talking about, telling me he himself was here in Cheyenne for the same exact reason, helpfully adding that there

was "no work at all down in Florida," where he was originally from.

Using a bicycle-pump-looking thing, he did a test on the radiator to see what was wrong with it. He removed the cap and, after a couple pumps, told me that the entire radiator was shot, explaining why—it was cracked all along the top, and I could plainly see that fluid was just pouring out of it. He said I needed a new one. I told him fine, and he went to get his boss, this older guy with a handlebar mustache who I assumed was Buck. My guy relayed the problem to him, and after a couple phone calls, I was given an estimate: $350. Plus tax.

I asked how fast they could get it done, and he said by five that evening, or I could pick it up the following morning at six. I handed him the keys and told him I'd more than likely pick it up in the morning.

.

Several hours later I was about to hop over a chain-link fence to go explore this tall abandoned cement building over by the *Wyoming Tribune* to see what was inside, perhaps take some arty pictures, when my cell phone started to vibrate. Since it was a 306 area code, I picked up. It was the lady from the labor temp agency; she had a job for me to go out on, if I was interested. I told her I was, and asked what kind of work it was. She told me, "Demolition work."

I lied and told her I could get there in about fifteen minutes or less. She said that was perfect, ending the call, "See you soon."

The only way I could get to the location in fifteen would be by driving, and since the Caliente was in the shop, that wasn't an option. My other options were to hitchhike, like Kerouac, or take a cab. Since Cheyenne is not downtown San Francisco, where you could track down a cab relatively easily, my best bet was to run or walk as fast as I could, on the side of the road, with my thumb out, hoping some kind soul would give me a lift. This never happened. What happened was, everybody passed by me. Desperate not to lose this job, I decided to stop at a Kum & Go gas station, where two guys were standing out in front, smoking. One looked like an employee having a smoke break, the other like an automobile owner. When I asked the guy who looked like an automobile owner whether he would be willing to give me a ride for a couple bucks, he told me that he couldn't because he didn't own a car. The guy manning the store told me that I could use the phone inside to call a cab, and that they're usually pretty fast about showing up. So I did, and the dispatcher told me that it'd take about ten minutes for the cab to arrive.

Standing by the pay phones, waiting for my cab, I set my backpack on the ground, leaned up against the wall, and lit a cigarette—I was feeling good, minutes away from being employed. A station wagon slowly pulled into the parking lot, and two early-twenties hipster-looking girls got out. They both looked straight out of an Urban Outfitters catalog, one with an SLR digital camera around her neck, kind of hot, in that arty-farty kind of way. I thought this was slightly odd for Cheyenne, but didn't think much about it as I quickly went back to daydreaming about how cool it was that I got a job doing demolition work. Just like in *Good Will Hunting*!

The two girls chatted for a second, and I could tell the one with the camera really wanted to say something. Finally, she did. She even used the word *please*. She asked if she could take a picture of me.

I looked up and down at what I was wearing, wondering if there was something wrong or funny going on, since that's the only time, really, I ever want to take a photo of someone I don't know. I was wearing low-top Chuck Taylors, white socks, thrashed gray Dickies, and a vintage early-1960s Pendleton flannel shirt. Accessories: knockoff Ray-Ban Wayfarers. Taking a drag, I told her, "Um, yeah, sure. Go ahead."

The girl snapped a couple quick snapshots of me, and then thanked me. She hesitated, debating whether to add anything more to that statement, finally going ahead and saying, "You look like you're going somewhere."

I smiled.

•

I was informed I needed three items for this job: work boots, work gloves, and safety glasses. When I showed the lady my sunglasses, she thought about it for a second, then decided they would be sufficient. Since I didn't have boots and gloves, I was issued a set, just like in the military. The first pair of work gloves were free, she told me, but after that, I'd have to pay fifty cents per pair. Just like toilet paper at the hotel. The work boots were loaners, which I had to sign for and return at the end of the day.

I brought the boots over to one of the white plastic

chairs, removing my scuffed-up Chucks, inserting my feet into the boots. These boots were dark brown, kind of like the old desert tan ones I had in Iraq, with my blood type written in Sharpie on the side. There's a certain technique to tying up the laces to your boots in the military: you loop the lace around, tie it off, and tuck it in. I instinctively did the same thing with these boots.

I soon found myself sitting in the back seat of a shitty Mitsubishi, while the two guys seated in the front seats discussed global warming. The guy giving us a ride to the job site worked for the company; the guy seated in the front passenger seat was a redheaded fortysomething with a thick midwestern accent, and we'd be working together. I quickly found that he liked to use the words *fuck* and *shit* in every sentence at least once or twice. Like, "Fuck this shit." And he went on and on telling the driver, who was agreeing with him, that global warming is just a bunch of bullshit, and that what he doesn't understand is that if carbon dioxide is actually good for plants, then the more carbon dioxide in the air, the more plants will grow. Guy talked like he was a scientist, but I didn't think he was.

Back in San Francisco, words like *Walmart*, *Starbucks*, *nonrecyclable*, *corporation*, *SUV*, etc. are all considered dirty words, but what I'm noticing is that the closer you get to Middle America, the less you hear about those being the dirty words. Here, words such as *environmentalists*, *Obama*, *socialism*, *light beer*, and *fat-free* are the dirty ones.

·

For whatever reason, Safeway had decided to postpone building a new Safeway. That's fine, but since Safeway had already purchased this lot with several abandoned houses sitting on it, our job was to help clean up the area, board up all the windows and doors of all the houses and trim the trees. They wanted the lot, and the vacant houses, to look somewhat decent so as to not bring down the property values of the surrounding homes.

When we got to the job site, a pickup with Colorado plates was parked in the middle of the lot, where two guys were already hard at work sawing sheets of plywood. There was a Mexican guy in his forties, perfect English, and a twentysomething named Tyrone. Tyrone was the first Tyrone I'd ever met who was not black. We shake hands, and the Mexican guy, who is in charge of this operation, takes both me and the other guy I'm working with all around the lot, explaining the job to us. To me, this is not demolition work at all, but more mortuary affairs for the six turn-of-the-century homes that now sit vacant on the lot, waiting to one day be cremated to make way for a bigger, better Super Safeway.

As the guy in charge walks us around, I noticed that one of the houses had EAST SIDE spray-painted on the side, another, the word CRIP in blue. Why is it that the two jobs I've gotten on this trip so far have both been in neighborhoods with gang graffiti? Also, I don't even know, but isn't it supposed to be Crips, not Crip? Is there only one Crip here in Cheyenne, Wyoming?

It had been a while since I took wood shop in high school, so I was going to go ahead and offer to do the gardening, but since the guy I was working with made a beeline straight to the woodcutting and paint, I didn't have much of a choice in the matter. I decided I was indeed in charge of cutting down all the shrubbery and trees. I wondered if he did that on purpose because he knew how much of a fucking pain in the ass it was doing that kind of work. I told the guy in charge that I'd go ahead and start on the greenery. He said, "Great," and handed me a chain saw.

Chain saws are easy, right? You just pull the cord and it starts up, just like in *Texas Chain Saw Massacre*, right? After about twenty or thirty pulls on the cord, I started to realize that I was doing something wrong, probably missing a step or two in getting this thing on. I didn't want to go over to where the other guys were and ask them how to start it up, for fear of being laughed at, so I pulled out my iPhone and called the 800 number on top of the chain saw, provided in case you have any questions. I figured if that didn't work, there had to be some sort of eHow.com article on the subject.

It seems there was a plastic bubble on top of the chain saw that I was supposed to press to allow fuel in. After I did that a few times, it fired right up. Loud.

With my brand-new work gloves on, handling a gas-powered chain saw spewing toxic carbon dioxide into the Wyoming atmosphere, Beethoven's Ninth Symphony in D Minor playing in my head, I immediately felt at one with the saw as I started cutting down every single fucking thing that was green, throwing the saw passionately left and right, up and down. With each violent swing of the saw, a cloud of green leaves, branches, and twigs exploded in all directions around me. It was beautiful.

With the sun burning my skin, I can feel sweat pouring down my face, and my arms feel like they're turning into lead weights. I keep on going. A couple times I have to take a break since sweat mixed with dirt is stinging my eyes. I use my T-shirt to wipe myself off, and get straight back to work.

I was working off pure adrenaline, sawing, cutting, swinging, chomping, branch by branch, twig by twig, every now and then a piece of branch backfiring, piercing my skin, drawing blood. I would exact my revenge, no green left behind.

The boss finally came out to see my work, commenting, "Wow. You took down all those trees nicely." He bought us all pizza, and during our break, we stood around under the shade of a house eating. I found out the two guys from Colorado travel all over, wherever the jobs are, and live at a motel packed with other people who come here for work. The one guy tells me that a lot of people in Cheyenne are from Michigan. He said he feels sorry for a few that he knows because they've been away from home for a while, stuck in Cheyenne while their families stay in Michigan.

After that, it was back to work. They had a huge steel Dumpster set up in the middle of the lot, and my job for the next several hours, as well as the next several days, should I so choose, was to pile all the clippings I had created into a wheelbarrow, roll it over to the Dumpster, dump it, repeat.

Singing, "Sixteen Tons," by Merle Travis, I kept on loading, and by the end of the day, I felt like I had loaded sixteen tons into that Dumpster. I had no idea that deforestation work could be so demanding. But before I could go home for the day, there was one last task. I had to destroy the white picket fence surrounding one of the houses.

Exhausted, my white undershirt no longer white, my skin a shade more olive than when I began, I stood there in front of the white picket fence with my work gloves on, cigarette dangling from my sweaty lips. I thought for a second about what tools I was going to use, and how I was going to tear this thing down.

I decided to go hand-to-hand on the fucker. It's a far more intimate way to destroy something than by using fancy machinery or tools. I flicked my smoke to the side and went animalistic on the fence, armed with nothing but brute force and willpower, work gloves and combat boots— I mean work boots. While I was on the ground, tearing it apart, grunting, I looked up to see a kid on a bicycle staring at me with his head cocked to the side, kind of how a dog does when he's confused. I wanted to tell the kid that this is what happens when you don't go to college, but he just gave me a perplexed look and pedaled off. I went back to what I was doing, and when I was finished, there was nothing but slivers and bits of the white fence scattered all over the ground around me, like bones scattered after a pack of wolves have angrily devoured something big. Maybe a moose.

Now that the workday was over, a different guy from the labor agency came by to pick us up. I sat down in the back seat, way too exhausted to pay any attention to the two guys seated in the front, who talked to each other the whole way back. I just smoked, staring out the window blankly, not really thinking about anything. I was too drained to think.

After handing in our time sheets, I returned my boots and was offered the option of getting paid by check or by cash. The guy I had been working with selected cash, as did I, and a couple minutes later we were handed sheets of paper with a series of numbers to enter into the ATM-like machine in the back. He went first. The machine dispensed his money; he counted it, placed the cash in his jeans, and went to the restroom to take a piss. I went over, typed in my digits, and while I was waiting for the money to shoot out of it, I saw a sign above reminding us to please pay our drivers. After I got my money, all $34.63 of it, I just kind of stood there, wondering if there was more money to come, but nothing else came out. The machine worked perfectly fine. When I turned around to ask about the "Please Pay Your Driver" sign, I was informed that for each ride to or from work, you have to pay that driver $2 in cash. I paid the guy who drove me back, which left me with a hard-earned $32.63 for the day. Only $390 more, and I'd have my radiator all paid off.

We both walked out at the same time, saying "See you tomorrow" to each other. The sun was about to set, and I watched as he limped east on foot while holding his flannel shirt over his right shoulder. I limped west, my flannel shirt over my right shoulder, too.

•

Back at the hotel, a really pale, skinny, shirtless guy stopped me once I got to the top of the stairs. He was holding a miniature electric fan, asking if I was interested in purchasing it off him. I told him no, not today. Limping to my room, exhausted, I opened the door, glad to see that nobody had broken into it to steal any of my shit. I lit a smoke, cracked open another bottle of wine, turned on the television, sat back in the old chair. Beat, I drank the wine straight out of the bottle, catching up on today's news with CNN. Before passing out, I set the alarm on my cell phone to 5:45 a.m.

When I woke up, I grabbed my complimentary roll of toilet paper and walked over to the "gentlemen's" toilet down the hall, half asleep and fully hung over. I took a shit, and returned to my room. I was still dressed, so I grabbed my pack of smokes and my work gloves up from the red carpet, and left. While walking toward the stairs, I found myself fixated on the old dusty American flag hung in the hallway. As I approached, it kind of woke me up, reminding me again what it is like to be an American: no health care, long hours of hard work, shit pay, and nothing to show for it while you make other people in air-conditioned offices richer and richer. As I went down the two flights of stairs, a guy sitting in a chair at the bottom just silently stared.

Instead of making a left toward the parking garage, I made a right, down East Lincolnway, on my way back to Buck's to grab my car before work. When I got there at 6:45 a.m., I asked Buck if the car was done; it was. As I handed him my debit card, I asked if the car needed a tune-up, since I was pretty sure the guy who sold it to me hadn't given it one since the 1960s. I explained that since I started heading east from Salt Lake City, I had noticed that sometimes when I tried to start her up, I had to turn the ignition several times, which never really happened back in California. He told me that what was probably going on was that the altitude was messing up the engine. He suggested that I wait on getting a tune-up until I was at least two hundred miles east of here, closer to sea level. If he did a tune-up here, the car would be kind of screwed once I leveled out in Nebraska. "I started the car and drove it into the garage myself," he said. "The engine sounded fine to me."

When I signed the receipt for the new radiator, I saw that the total was $410. At the rate I was being paid, I'll have to demolish stuff for nearly a month to pay it off. I shake Buck's hand, thanking him for his work, and drive the Caliente back around the corner, parking just out of view of the day labor office.

•

The lady behind the counter greeted me as I signed in, asking whether I was going to need a cash advance today to pay my driver. Jesus, there are people in this country willing to do hard day labor who don't have a measly two bucks on them so that they can even get work? My God. I told the lady that wasn't necessary today, that I had just gotten my car back from the shop, and I'd be able to drive both myself and the guy I was working with to and from the worksite today.

Just like the day before, about a dozen or so people were patiently waiting for work on white plastic chairs or milling around outside, some seated on the hoods of rusty old cars parked along the curb. I wondered how many of them might have dream boards. One of the guys I had worked with the other day was seated on the bus bench, a crowd gathered around him. I got the impression he was somewhat popular; they were all listening to him intensely, every now and then erupting in laughter as his stories continued.

Back inside, I filled my Styrofoam cup with some coffee, mixed in a little powdered creamer, and took a seat next to two women. One woman was shaped like a pear and had a short haircut. I later found out she worked full-time at a fast food joint, on her days off coming down here in her pickup to jump on day-labor gigs. She asked the woman next to her, slightly younger, if she had ever read a book called *The Purpose Driven Life*. The younger woman told her that a friend of hers had actually recommended the book, but for whatever reason she hadn't gotten around to it. I'd never heard of it, but I liked the title, so added it to my mental book queue.

I stepped outside for another smoke to go along with my coffee, and walked into a conversation as to which prepaid cell phone service was the best, and which ones sucked ass. The lady standing in the center of the group, wearing sweatpants and a hoodie, was leaning up against a car telling everybody about how her mother purchased her one of these prepaid cell phones, so that she could call her and her grandkids whenever she wanted to talk to them, but that she couldn't afford the prepaid service, so it was useless.

"I live in a hotel, okay? I got that and three kids to feed; food stamps ain't cutting it, which is why I'm working here so I can make some extra cash. You know, instead of a phone, I could use that fifty bucks to help feed my kids and, like, buy milk."

I returned to my spot next to the two women inside, the younger one now telling the pear-shaped one all about how "he" grabbed her arms really hard, so hard that he left bruises on them, and after that, he proceeded to bite her real hard in the rib cage area—"that's a pretty sensitive area, even for a guy"—leaving a deep bite mark, and after biting her, "he just kept on punching me over and over again, and I was like, you are way too controlling."

I looked up at the clock. It was getting close to game time, so I wandered back outside over to the bus stop where the guy I worked with was still entertaining the crowd, to let him know that it was time for us to go. Surprisingly, he remembered my name. "Hey, Colby, you ready for another fucking day of bullshit or what?"

Amazed that he remembered my name, I enthusiastically told him that I was. I had forgotten his name. I remembered what the guy I met in Green River, Wyoming, had told me about people here in the middle of the country remembering names.

Once we'd received our time cards and stepped outside, I told him I was parked around the corner. When we got closer to the Caliente, he said, "Shit man, this is yours?"

I told him it was, and he got excited, especially when he saw the California plates. He asked if it was a California car, and I told him that I had driven her all the way here. When he got inside he commented that it smelled like it had been stored in a garage for years; I was amazed that the guy could still smell, since he smokes about a carton a day. As I started the car up, I told him that I had purchased it off a guy who claimed to have gotten it from his grandfather, the original owner.

Since he knew the town better than I did, I asked him for directions to where we needed to be. He told me to make a left at the stop sign. I paused—I didn't want to make a left.

All my life I've liked to wear muted monotone colors, blacks and grays. Aside from acknowledging that you can't tell when they're dirty, I had never thought anything of this color scheme of mine other than how I liked the way those tones looked on me, until my sister brought it up. She said I liked wearing "depressing" colors because I don't like to draw any attention to myself, that people who wear bright colors are more confident. She mentioned that I needed to wear brighter colors more often, which I ignored. A left turn would mean that I would have to drive right in front of the vehicle-less people standing around the agency. Well, this was the direction we had to go. What were the chances that the people outside would notice us driving by?

As soon as we rolled by, with the window rolled down, my passenger yelled out, "Hey, guys!" Everybody looked up. I kept my head down, embarrassed, as he yelled, "Check out the wheels, huh?!" He had a huge smile as we drove away. To me, they all just looked confused as we drove off, but he seemed to be having a blast. Since all the windows were rolled down, at the first red light, he asked the car next to us if they wanted to race for pink slips. "You wish you had this car, don't you?" He threw his head back and laughed as the light turned green and the two of us headed toward work.

I now knew exactly what I felt like. I felt like that dorky kid in high school that got to hang out with the cool kids because of his car. I was the guy with no personality, who obtained popularity thanks to his wheels. This depressed me.

"This job's not too bad, man," he told me as we drove along. "I've been on some shit jobs, and this ain't one of them. You know what I had to do on the last bullshit job that they sent me out on? I had to move fucking rocks, man, all fucking day long, man. I had to move them from one spot over to another. I'm a fucking union man. I used to make pretty fucking good money until the economy took a shit, a couple hundred dollars a day. Now I can't get shit, fucking Obama, man, fuck him, he's the reason I'm doing this shit."

●

A portable stereo was plugged in at the job site today, turned to a classic rock station. I continued my project, decimating trees and bushes, wheeling the carnage away in a wheelbarrow, eventually moving on to boarding up windows on the abandoned homes. It was good listening to the Stones, Zeppelin, and Jimi. "(I Can't Get No) Satisfaction" came on, and it seemed to boost our morale, which was sad, but also kind of sweet. I found out the name of the guy I was working with, Dave, as he came up to me several times during breaks, always starting the conversation by telling me in some form or another about how he used to be a union worker, making pretty good coin.

"Winter's coming up, man, ain't no fucking way I am going to work out in the fucking cold again this winter, fuck that shit, man. I'm going to get myself a job indoors at a restaurant, man, know what I'm saying? You can make some pretty good money doing that shit, working in a restaurant."

Nodding in agreement, I told him, "Yeah, you can make good tips doing that," just trying to do my part in the conversation. Head slightly cocked, he looked at me all confused, like I was reading from the wrong page. "I'm talking McDonald's, man, or some pizza joint flipping pizzas."

"Oh, yeah."

"Yeah! You can make pretty good money doing that shit, they start you off at eight bucks an hour at some of those places, and it's indoors so I don't got to worry about freezing my ass off like I did last winter. I think I'm going to get myself a restaurant job. Fuck this shit, man; I used to be a union worker, you know?"

•

After a full eight hours of work, the day was over. Time cards completed, Dave and I drove back, got our money, and went back to our hotel rooms.

The wine I was drinking up in my room did not taste as good as it once did, so I decided to go out on a walk.

The guy I'd periodically noticed sitting outside the hotel was now sitting on an upside-down plastic bucket. He was a tall guy with a thick accent, sixty-two years old. He said, "Hello." We shook hands, and he introduced himself as Chuck. "My name is Chuck, and I don't give a fuck." With his thumb he points to the hotel and tells me that not a lot of people who live there care for him much. "But I don't give a fuck," he said.

He looked me up and down and asked where I was from. Unimpressed, he asked if I had ever done any time in prison. "I was in the army for a couple years," was my answer, and an enormous smile appeared as he told me that he had been a marine for eight years, afterward living on the streets for nine, and loved every minute of both. He loved hopping trains and even had a painting of a train up in his room, he loved it that much.

In front of the hotel was a bike rack filled with shitty bikes, many of which I assume belong to folks who have received one too many DUIs. Chuck told me a story of something that happened a couple nights before. He was outside smoking, where the two of us were now, and a drunk he knows from the neighborhood came along and started trying to steal one of the bikes. Now, he would have, except that he was so drunk off his ass that he kept on falling down to the ground every time he tried to pedal away. So Chuck called the cops, and they came on down and arrested the guy. While the guy was cuffed and stuffed in the back seat of the police car, he yelled at Chuck that when he got released the next day from jail, he was going to find him and stab him. Since the guy was threatening Chuck, the cops asked him if he wanted to press charges. Chuck proudly told me that he told the cops, "I've lived here at this hotel for years. If the worst thing that ever happened to me was somebody stabbing me, well then, I'm a pretty fucking lucky guy."

•

Work the next day started at 9:00 a.m. At 9:30 a.m., Tyrone pulled a pipe out from his jeans pocket, and a bunch of the guys all smoked marijuana. At 10:30 a.m., the boss arrived on the job site with an eighteen-pack of cheap beer. At 11:30 a.m., during a break, Dave pulled out a roach from his jeans pocket and passed that around. At 12:30 p.m. we were already out of beer, and since we had been drinking on empty stomachs, we all had nice beer buzzes going . . . so the boss took off to go pick up another eighteen-pack for us to consume. At 1:30 p.m., with nearly half the second eighteen-pack already gone, we were all sitting around on the porch of a partially boarded-up house, drinking what was left of the beers. Tyrone again pulled out his pipe and passed that around, asking why I didn't smoke. I told him I usually did, but I wasn't going to today because I'd driven to work. "Where's your ride at?" It was parked down the street under a huge tree for shade, and when I turned and pointed to it, he tapped his boss and said, "I told you!"

Told him what? He explained that the previous night while they were out drinking, he told our boss that I had some 1950s greaser thing going on with me, and that he could tell I was the kind of person who would be into older cars like that. I loathe being categorized. Must be the tattoos.

At around 4:30 p.m., the boss signed us out, logging 5:00 p.m. on our time cards. Tyrone was nearly passed out, lying on the ground like a beached whale. Dave and I headed back to the day labor agency. "Man, I'm fucking ripped," he said. He gave me some advice, which was not to talk too much when we got back, since if we did, they would smell the alcohol on our breath—and that I should let him do all the talking. When we got there I followed his instructions, and the only talking I did was stating my preference for being paid in cash.

•

I woke up in the morning the same way I had the past several days since working this job—hung over, with every single muscle in my body aching. I'm in my early thirties, in fairly decent shape, having worked out in the local YMCA every day for several months prior to this trip. Long hours in the driver's seat, gas station food, empty calories from beer and whiskey, had all contributed to the extra inch or two on my waistline and overall poor health at this point. I really did not want to go to work that day, but since Dave and I had agreed to work, and he was relying on me for a ride, I had to go. After a cold shower, I left the hotel, picked up a cup of coffee, and left to get Dave. Since it was Sunday, the office would be closed, but he would be waiting for me there.

It was Sunday, and early, so I assumed I'd be sharing the road with people on their way to church, since anybody who'd gone out drinking last night would probably still be in bed. I parked the car in front of the labor agency, sipping coffee, waiting for Dave. Finally, at 8:15 a.m., he showed up wearing his brown work boots, an old sun-faded Budweiser cap, blue jeans, and today a T-shirt with a huge rainbow trout on it. He also had a cup of gas station coffee in one hand, a cigarette in the other. He got in my car, and we set off on our way. Taking a sip from his coffee, I could tell by the expression on his face that it did not taste good today, and he said, "This coffee ain't cutting it for me this morning. You want to go to a bar and grab a couple beers before work?" I said sure, and when I asked where to, he guided me to the local VFW.

I don't think you necessarily have to be a veteran of a foreign war to drink at a VFW bar; all you need to be is an alcoholic. Dave had been in the army, enlisting after Vietnam, so he was a veteran, but not a veteran of a foreign war. Even though I was late on my membership fees, I am a proud card-carrying member of the VFW. I'm noticing that every midsize town has a VFW. You can hopscotch across this great country of ours, and never have to drink alone.

When we got to the VFW, the back parking lot was completely full. At 8:25 a.m., every single bar stool was taken, so we ordered a couple tall Bud Lights, bringing them out to the back patio, which was also a smoking section. I'm super paranoid about drunk driving, so I told myself that I would only drink half a beer, and then after that guzzle some coffee to cover up the smell in case I got pulled over. When my beer was empty, I looked over at Dave, and his beer was empty, too.

"Fuck it." He grimaced. "Do you really want to work today?" I didn't, and I could tell he didn't either. "No," I said. "I'm way too beat."

"Me, too. Fuck it, it's bullshit, we ain't getting paid shit. It's Sunday, and I'm a goddamn union worker, busting my ass all day long and then coming into the office afterward and ain't getting paid shit for it. Fuck 'em!" I nodded my head in agreement. "Here's what we'll do. I'll call them up and tell them that after you picked me up this morning we drove . . . all the way to Colorado . . . to buy lottery tickets! And the fucking car broke down! And we're stuck!"

Maybe he was still drunk from the night before. "You think they'll believe that?"

"Yeah! Check it out, Colorado is only about seven miles away, and you can't buy lottery tickets in Wyoming! The only place you can get 'em around here is Colorado!"

This guy was fucking awesome. Seriously, Dave was great. I could never have made that shit up. So I picked up the next round while he pulled out his cell phone to leave a message telling them that we were broken down somewhere in Colorado purchasing lottery tickets at eight fucking thirty in the morning on a Sunday. On my way to the bar, I stopped by the bathroom to take a piss and noticed two jittery Mexicans, one in full cowboy garb, the other busy taking a long piss in a urinal. I could hear a long "sniff" going on from the stall next to me.

Back where Dave was, I sat around and chatted with a guy who rolled up to the VFW on his mountain bike. He said that his profession was freelance tree cutter. We talked shop for a bit. I told him about my job, he told me about his, and I noticed that several of the discussions around me were about DUIs. I was shocked to find that almost everyone around me had at least one or two stories, many times beginning with, "My first DUI, I was . . ." I had suspected that was why a lot of them rolled up to the VFW on bicycles. This made me nervous again, and after about five or six beers each, I thought it'd be better for me to grab a bite to eat. I stepped downstairs, where they served breakfast, and purchased a breakfast burrito with a side of hash browns for six bucks. I scarfed that down, and went back up to the smoking section. I told Dave that I was exhausted and was going to go home to take a nap—if he needed a ride, I'd give him one. He borrowed ten bucks from a friend of his, and on the way to his motel—taking side streets, since there'd probably be fewer cops—he asked if I could do him a huge favor and pull into a liquor store real quick. I said sure, and while I waited for him in the car, three guys sitting outside the store drinking and smoking stared long and hard at me. Finally, one of them, a guy wearing a mesh hat yelled out, "What engine you got in there?" I got out of the car, motioned them over, and lifted up the hood, showing them the engine, and we talked cars for a bit. When Dave showed back up with a bottle in a brown paper sack, he told them, "You gotta love them California cars, huh?"

When I dropped Dave off at his motel, he told me that on Monday, when I showed back up to work, I should give him my number, so that we could hang out more often. I told him sure thing.

•

The next morning, I walked over to Room 101 and knocked on the door. Joe answered, and I told him that I was leaving. Joe handed my $5 deposit back. "Where you off to next?" he asked.

"Denver."

CHAPTER SEVEN

Life After Last Call

"There's no place like home."

DOROTHY,
The Wizard of Oz

He started off by asking me three questions:

"Do you have a valid ID?"

"Do you have any warrants out for your arrest?"

"Are you a registered sex offender?"

I answered no to two out of the three, handing over my driver's license. He handed me some paperwork to fill out, which I did on a chair in the lobby next to half a dozen garbage bags filled with clothes. He told me I could have whatever I wanted out of those bags. It was clothing from people who had moved out of the hotel without paying or saying good-bye, which happens a lot. "People just leave," he told me. "You can sometimes find some good stuff." I looked through a couple of the bags to see if there was anything in them that I could possibly sell over at Buffalo Exchange, which I saw was a couple blocks away; I could use the money for gas. There wasn't anything worth taking, or selling, or even donating.

After handing him $33 for the room, I was given keys and a new location to call home. The room was a bit more than I had been paying in Cheyenne, but this was Denver, a city with a slightly higher cost of living than the cities I had been visiting. The room was definitely bigger, equipped with a small television, a chair, and a table with, of course, an ashtray. Like Cheyenne, no bathroom or shower; those were communal and located somewhere down the hall. No art was hung on the walls.

There was also something missing. This hotel felt as if there was no soul; it felt dead. It didn't feel as lively as the hotel in Cheyenne, and I got the impression that it was just another building with rooms with beds in them, nothing more. While sitting on the bed, I wondered what I should do. I looked out the window, and across the street was a bar. The patrons all appeared to be young and well-dressed. It was like every other bar, in every other city, scattered across the country.

Somebody dropped a bottle, it smashed on the ground. People reacted by applauding and cheering.

I made my way over to my bed, a quick prayer to the Lord Almighty that the bed I rest upon tonight be minus bedbugs. Closing my eyes, I went to sleep.

The next morning, I made my way to the airport. After dropping the mistress off over in long-term parking, complete with farewell kiss good-bye, I stepped onto a white shuttle van. The driver asked me what airline. I told him United. He closed the door behind me, I took a seat. Staring out the window, I watched as the driver navigated through the lot. I wondered what the chances were of my plane crashing on the way to my destination.

CHAPTER EIGHT

The North Will Rise Again

"If you speak of the tiger, it will come."

KOREAN PROVERB

호랑이도 제 말하면 온다

While on this adventure, we had agreed that my wife would take our newborn son back to where she had grown up in southern Ohio, where her parents would be able to spend time with him and help her through his first few months. Now that I'd been gone for a while, it was clear she needed me, and I wanted to see my son.

When I arrived, not only did she look just as dangerously beautiful as before, but I noticed immediately that my wife had changed, dramatically. She seemed numb, thousand-yard stare, thick bags under her eyes. She seemed somewhere else, and it didn't take me long to find out why. That first night was spent with my son waking screaming, crying, every thirty minutes. She breastfed him, handing him off for a diaper change as needed. If he was still screaming postmeal, my job was either to rock him to sleep sitting in the rocking chair or strap him into a BabyBjörn, walking him around the room until he was able to calm down. Now, it's not that easy. Just because he falls asleep, or even stops crying, doesn't mean he's going to stay that way. You have to continue rocking or walking him for a good thirty minutes until he's pretty much in a coma, and then, gently, like defusing an IED, slowly place him back into bed. If he wakes up at any point in this process, you have to start over, completely. In those rare times he did end up asleep, it wasn't long before he would wake up, ready to start the entire cycle all over again. That first night, I would be surprised if I had slept two hours total.

.

My wife likes to cook, that's her thing. She had planned to cook up an Italian dinner, needing some prosciutto for the particular dish she had in mind. We drove a good thirty minutes away to one of the only Italian stores in the area, only to find out that they didn't have any. Frustrated, my wife told me that this was why she could never live here. Back in San Francisco, you could find this easily. Here, in southern Ohio, you can't find shit.

So on the way back we decided to stop by Walmart, compromising on our dinner ingredients. In the parking lot, I noticed that the vehicle parked next to us had two baby seats in the back. That's just insane to me, having one kid right after the other. I put my son into the BabyBjörn, and as we made our way to the entrance, I saw a teenage couple, child in tow. I asked my wife if she thought that was their kid, and she told me that people around there like to have kids really young. Once inside, we passed another teenage couple who had two kids with them. What was strange to me was that me and my wife, both in our thirties, probably looked like the old couple who decided to have kids way later on in life. Back in San Francisco, we look like the misfits having kids way too early.

For whatever reason, I am intrigued by Walmart. I understand the attraction to a large superstore, I do—shoppers can rely on both diversity and availability of product, and can count on a certain level of service, these things not varying all too much across the country other than satisfying certain regional expectations. Like whole aisles of tortillas in California. Personally, I prefer to support mom-and-pop operations, but that's sometimes hard when you don't know where to find them, or just need to know that when you walk in, there will be the opportunity to buy not only a cooler, ice, and beer, but toothpaste and diapers. I understand why America shops here—it's easy.

I've noticed this in other Walmarts, too, but if you look at their salad dressing selection, the fat-free or low-fat dressing always seems to be fully stocked, like nobody has ever touched them. The full-flavor, full-calorie, full-fat salad dressing is always more picked over. As I was pointing this out to my wife, a hefty lady wearing sweats pulled her cart up and grabbed two large containers of regular ranch dressing. None of the items in her cart gave any indication that she was on any particular diet. Walmart gives the option of fat-free, low-fat food, but if the consumer chooses not to purchase it, whose fault is that?

As my wife and I were discussing that over by the produce section, she spotted her prosciutto. Walmart had it.

•

Summer in Middle America means county fair season, and what I've come to find is that these fairs are the very last place in the world you'll want to go if you're on a diet. Trying to recover from some of the damage I'd done the past few weeks traveling, I was unable to eat any of the food that they were selling, since they all seemed to be in the million-calories-per-serving category. Figuring that despite its sugar content it was still a better choice than a couple of deep-fried Oreos, I bought some lemonade off a black man working a stand. I looked around and realized that he was the only black man there, and that everybody else, except me, was white. We were the only minority "brothers" at the county fair.

My wife reminded me, again, that I'm not a "brother," and that this was also one of the reasons she had left home as soon as she could, and why she could never move back, nor ever choose to raise children here. There is no diversity. Everybody is white. She had a point, but the trade-off, I told her, was that if I was a kid, I would have loved this county fair. There were farm animals all over the place, a roller coaster, junk food, and everyone looked like they were really enjoying themselves. We have county fairs in California, but there was something different about the vibe here, only miles from West Virginia.

Passing by a souvenir stand, I noticed a cool mesh cap with the Confederate flag embroidered on the front of it. I noticed several other people at the county fair had on Confederate flag hats and T-shirts, and I thought it was kind of odd that people here in Ohio were wearing them, since the last time I checked, Ohio is a little north to be considered the South. I picked up one of the hats, looked at the label—"Made in China"—and put it on to see how it fit. While I was looking in the mirror, my wife, who was checking out all the T-shirts on the wall with silk-screened deer, turned around in horror as she saw what I was wearing. She immediately told me to take it off and put it back on the rack.

"Why? It's cool there, and the people are nice. What's wrong with a half-Asian combat veteran from California wearing a Confederate flag mesh cap? I like the South."

She then explained to me that the Confederate flag means something entirely different around these parts, that it's a redneck thing and that the people here who wear Confederate flag merchandise made in China wear it for redneck pride, and that a lot of them have probably never been to the South, ever. "It's a symbol of ignorance and racism," she said.

I pulled out my wallet.

"What are you doing?!"

"I'm going to get it."

"Don't you dare!"

Why not? I explained to her that if more minorities wore Confederate flags, then maybe it would lose some of its redneck power. I've been to the South, I like it there, people are cool, and the food's good. She told me that's great, but pointed out that the South also wanted to keep slavery going.

Fair enough. I put the hat back on the rack and asked, "So, what else is there to check out here at the county fair?"

•

The night before I left Ohio, I stepped outside for a cigarette. While smoking, I could hear the cars on the nearby freeway tear by, people inside—leaving somewhere, going somewhere.

I wonder what's going to happen to me when I get off this road.

CHAPTER NINE

Never Look Back

"Travel is fatal to prejudice, bigotry, and narrow-mindedness, and many of our people need it sorely on these accounts. Broad, wholesome, charitable views of men and things cannot be acquired by vegetating in one little corner of the earth all one's lifetime."

MARK TWAIN

Once again reunited with my mistress, I thought she looked more stunning than ever. We embraced, and amazingly, she fired up, first try. I let the engine run for a bit; it felt good to be back behind the wheel, like sitting back down on an old comfy sofa in your living room after a long day of work. When I shifted the car into reverse to exit long-term parking and pick up where I had left off, I noticed that my fuzzy dice were missing . . . as well as the rearview mirror from which they had been dangling. I looked around and saw that the mirror must have fallen off somehow, probably from being parked in the Denver sun too long.

Despite my love for the romantic symbolism of not being able to ever look back, I found out rather quickly that driving without a rearview is a lot more difficult than you might think. What you don't realize is how often you look behind you while driving, to see where you've been, or maybe to see whether any police are tailing you. Since this was now impossible for me to do, I became a bit paranoid and unable to concentrate on driving, so I pulled off the road and took side streets until I came across a small town with, of course, a twenty-four-hour Walmart, and small string of chain hotels nearby.

The next morning, since I don't like paying full price for shit, I made sure to help myself to a generous array of items from my motel's free continental breakfast—bagels, oranges, bananas, hard-boiled eggs—and stuffed them into my mini-cooler full of ice for snacking on the road. At a nearby AutoZone, I purchased a new rearview mirror, attaching it in their parking lot. Now able to see the road behind me, I felt a bit of comfort as I again headed east.

After being stranded in some small butt-fuck town thanks to a blown car generator, then a couple hundred miles later stranded again in another small butt-fuck town once that generator caught on fire, I ended up in Omaha, Nebraska.

•

The senior citizen working behind the desk at the hotel worked behind glass. He had on an old faded Cornhusker football T-shirt. I asked about vacancies. He told me that they had a room, and asked whether I was interested in a night or a week. I asked for prices on both. $25 a night, $90 for the week. $10 key deposit. I told him I'd take the week.

The door key was for Room 18, up on the second floor, and he explained to me that after three weeks, I'd be considered a resident, and the rent would go down to only $80 a week. There was a cigarette machine behind the front desk; I was all out, so I asked for a pack. They sold GPCs only, five bucks, so I bought a pack and made my way upstairs to my room. Four white walls, a bed, a sink with an old mirror above it, and an old wooden dresser drawer from the 1970s. That's it. No television or fridge. There were several bathrooms on each floor, which appeared to be clean. I only saw a couple cockroaches, and they weren't big, about the size of raisins. After storing my belongings in my room, I locked up and decided to take a walk.

Across the street from the aged hotel was some kind of hipster/punk rock frat Animal House that clearly belonged to a landlord who was like, *Fuck it, they can do whatever the hell they want, I don't care.* Shoes hanging from the telephone wires in front, dozens of cheap beer cans littered all over the place, a couple shattered windows, graffiti on the sidewalk, and a lawn decorated with a half-dozen thrashed skateboards sticking up out of the ground like tombstones.

I ended up at the bar next door. As I took a seat at the bar, "Bela Lugosi's Dead" by the band Bauhaus played from the jukebox. Two bucks and some change for a beer. Nice. The wall in the back had painted portraits on canvas of Johnny Rotten, Joey Ramone, Nick Cave, and Iggy Pop. The tables in the back were all filled with hipsters. I asked myself, Am I back in San Francisco, or am I in Omaha, Nebraska? The two seemed blurred, and the person next to me was wearing a Dead Kennedys T-shirt, with a mullet. I ordered a couple more beers, noticing that everybody here seemed to be either in a band or were just standing around waiting for Coachella. Many times I'd pass by a conversation on my way to the restroom, past the painted portrait of Hunter S. Thompson, of course, and some guy would be trying to impress some young thing with some crazy tour story. I stepped outside for a smoke, where I came across a white guy who looked like a continuation high school graduate. He sized me up and started off by telling me that he had just been released from prison. Lovely. I told him congratulations, not sure if I was supposed to be intimidated or impressed; I was neither. I was ambivalent, which I think confused him, and he asked me what I was up to tonight. I told him I was just traveling, seeing where the road takes me, and that I'd just moved into the hotel next door.

He lit up and told me that he also lived in the same building, which gave us a common bond instantly. He asked what I was doing at *that* bar. I shrugged, not knowing why or why not—told him I just was. Disgusted, he told me that the place was for "dorks," and, in a louder tone for all to hear, "faggots," suggesting that the two of us should go to a different bar instead. Not having any other plans, or ideas, I agreed to go with him, as I was curious what his angle was. I discovered exactly what it was when he asked me to buy him a beer, since he was broke.

A block or two away, we got situated in a different bar that, like the one I'd just left, lacked diversity; in this case, because we were the only two non-blacks there. A couple pool tables were set up in the middle of the place as soul music played from the sound system. At one of the tables was a guy wearing a purple suit, fedora, and multiple chains around his neck, playing pool with a younger guy dressed in baggy jeans and an equally baggy white T-shirt.

After I'd purchased my new friend a beer, he confessed that he hadn't actually just got out of prison; he just told people that as part of his hustle to get a couple bucks or a beer or two. How he really ended up here in Omaha, and at the hotel, was that he was working this job as a carny, going from one county fair to another, when he got into an argument with his manager's wife or something "over something dumb," so finally they fired him. Hello, Omaha.

•

I asked about day labor work, and he turned sour, advising me not to do that, that they put all the people that have been there for a while on all the jobs first, and it might take weeks before they put me on a job. *If* they put me on a job.

He then had an idea. Was I interested in going in with him on some weed? He had this connection, and the two of us could make some pretty good money going around selling weed to people. I told him sales had never been my strong suit. After a couple beers, he then suggested I do what he did, which was to go down to this building not too far from where we were and apply for food stamps. "They give you a card, and that card is like a credit card, you can buy food with it, as long as it's not hot food—$200 worth!"

Holy shit. $200 is a lot of groceries. I don't know if I could eat that much. I could live like a king off that, and probably get fat, though when I briefly did the math in my head, fifty bucks a week is hardly anything and I probably could lose a lot of weight on that particular diet but I told him I wasn't interested in food stamps right now.

When I exited the hotel bright and early the next morning, my friend was outside wearing a Dan Marino football jersey, which clashed with his Milwaukee Brewers cap. He was standing outside the hotel eating a steaming bowl of instant ramen for breakfast, with a plastic fork. He asked if I wanted to go to the bar to watch the football game, but I told him I had stuff to do, such as, find a job.

•

I took my sweet time looking for a job, as none of the jobs I came across looked even remotely interesting. Like everywhere else in the country, fast food restaurants were all hiring, but I was more interested in just bumming around Omaha, hung over, instead. The only job I applied for was one I came across on Craigslist:

> Drilling company is looking for hard working general laborers. Must be willing to travel. Will be out of town for 2 weeks then home for one week and so on.
>
> Shift: 1st
>
> Pay: $10-$12 (DOE)
>
> Hotel and food allowance provided when out of town.
>
> NO PHONE CALLS PLEASE. Due to the overwhelming amount of phone calls, we are asking that anyone who is interested, please come in and apply in person. Monday—Friday 8am—4pm

I shaved beforehand, thinking that it'd be competitive. The place was completely empty when I arrived. All the chairs in the waiting room sat empty, an overwhelming amount of nothing. After filling out all the paperwork, I asked how long it would take to hear back. The lady told me that there were a couple others who had turned in applications for a job, as well, and that I should hear back in a day or two for an interview. She handed me a card with her corporate head shot on it and told me that if I wanted to, I could call her to find out the status of my application. I thanked her and drove back to the room, took a nap, woke up, stared at the white paint on the walls, watched a tiny raisin walk across my carpet. Then I decided to go out and be productive.

·

Being productive while at the same time being unemployed actually takes a lot of work and is not as exciting, or as easy, as people might think.

For example, it took well over an hour for me to decide what I wanted to do today. Go on a walk? Where to? Go to a restaurant? Order fast food? I wasn't hungry. Drink? I could do that later, once the sun was down. I always prefer drinking when the sun's down; it makes me feel like less of an alcoholic. Watch a movie? Nothing interests me. Shop? I didn't need anything. Library? Maybe.

I then decided that I'd go to a bookstore instead. They always have the latest titles, and I had seen one earlier by the mall when I left the job placement place. I thought I'd just hang out there for a bit with a bunch of books other people have written.

Instead of driving, I decided to utilize Omaha public transportation. I always like to make an effort to take the bus whenever I'm in a new town because the bus, I feel, is truly a great way to experience the locals. In L.A., since everybody drives, crazy people take the bus. I'm talking absolutely schizo, pull foot powder out of the bag, open it up, and cloud up the entire bus with it kind of crazy. Bus lines can actually be like entering a war zone, especially right around the time school gets out and the bus is packed with kids cussing up a storm, grabbing each other, not caring in any way, shape, or form how many churchgoing grandmothers are seated around them. Immigrants on their way to their third or fourth job, the homeless guy drinking a tall can out of a brown paper bag bragging about how he knows Paris Hilton, or the guy hanging out the window smoking weed. Don't even bother trying to read on a bus in L.A. In other words, taking the bus can at times be like taking a walk on the wild side.

A tall, skinny black man in his fifties was standing there on the corner bus stop just outside the hotel, looking into the oncoming traffic.

"Where you headed?"

"To the mall."

"Which one?"

"The one on I think Seventy-second and Dodge."

"You need the number-two bus, that'll take you right there."

"Thanks."

"People don't really go to that mall anymore," he tells me as cars pass us by. "It's one of them dying malls, everybody's pulled out—Old Navy, Chili's—it's all empty inside. People don't like going there because the only people that

go there now are what you call them? Wannabe gang-
sters? So families don't go there no more. Everybody else
goes to them mega malls or superstores. Target's still there,
though, and they do okay, but that mall's on its way out.
They don't even got no food court. All that's gone now, too.
It's dead, man."

A bus came along, but it wasn't one either of us wanted.
He asked me what I was looking to get at the mall, since
most of the stores were no longer there, and I told him I
was just going to go to the bookstore. He told me that for
now, they were still there.

"We got a public library downtown you could go to,
but nobody goes there, either. That's dead, too. Everybody with a family goes to all them other libraries way
out there 'cause way too many homeless people hang out
there. Place is like a goddamn homeless shelter. One lady
told me she take her baby into the bathroom, and some
homeless lady was giving herself a bath in the sink! No
families want to see that shit, man, people shaving and
shit in the men's room, all smelling like ass sleeping up
in the library all day. Families don't want to see that shit,
man, so they don't go there no more. You know they got a
van that even shows up and gives them homeless people
free food and you know what happened? The hot dog guy
went out of business! Yeah! He ain't working no more. He
all out of business. Shit. I ain't got nothing against homeless people, if that's your thing then that's your thing,
but do it on your own time, in your own place, don't do it
at no motherfucking public library, you know what I'm
saying? Families go there. Either get yourself a hustle, or

get yourself a motherfucking job like the rest of us, you know what I'm saying?"

When I asked him how he ended up here in Omaha, he told me, "That's a long story. I was stationed for a bit in Germany, after that they sent me over by Tacoma, Washington—"

"Fort Lewis?"

"Yeah!"

"I was stationed there, too. Third Brigade."

"No shit?! Field artillery Twenty-fifth Division. Tropic Thunder."

Just then his bus arrived, so I never found out the story of how he ended up in Omaha. Before stepping onto the bus, he softly tapped his chest twice and raised his fist.

The number 2 arrived shortly thereafter. Like he said, the mall was completely dead, as was the parking lot, which sat empty. Inside was pretty vacant, but the bookstore was still open. After hanging out there for a bit, I got depressed, walked to a liquor store, purchased a bottle of whiskey, keeping it concealed in my jacket while periodically sipping from it as I walked back to the hotel.

I spent my last days in Omaha a drunken mess in my room.

> > > > >

CHAPTER TEN

Committed to Excellence

"You don't understand! I coulda had class.
I coulda been a contender. I coulda been somebody,
instead of a bum, which is what I am."

MARLON BRANDO,
On the Waterfront

I was a good hour's drive past the Nebraska-Iowa border
when I received the voice mail from *them*; I'd finally heard
back from the company offering that drilling job back in
Omaha. They had a job available for me, day labor, $9/
hour, a good fifty hours a week. I would have totally taken
the job, but the problem was, I'd already split town. I also
had a voice mail from the day labor agency back in Cheyenne, informing me that they also had a job available for
me. I thought about turning around and working these jobs
way off and over my rearview mirror's horizon, but I didn't
want to go backward, I needed to move forward. Onward.
Onward to . . . *victory*?

For me to receive a room in the beat hotel, another depressingly historic building in of course another historic
downtown, I had chosen in Des Moines, Iowa, it needed
to be verified that I was not on their 86'd list. The guy

working the desk pulled out an enormous file box filled with index cards of names, in alphabetical order, of people banned for life. Jesus, I told him, that's a lot of people. He told me, "That's nothing"—he's got four more boxes. He checked, didn't find my name, and told me that he had a corner room on the third floor available for a little over a hundred a week. I handed him the cash, and he laid all the twenties out on the counter, marking each one with his counterfeit pen.

"People are stupid, you'd be surprised how many come in here trying to rent a room with photocopied twenties."

"That happens a lot?"

"All the time."

Before handing me the key to Room 310, he kindly gave me a safety briefing. Since the ID I gave him was my California driver's license, head cocked, me arrogantly trying my hardest to give the *Officer, you have got to be fucking kidding me* face, he told me to be careful. "I used to live out in California, and I know how you people are— all laid-back—and you gotta be careful around here, some people might mistake that and try and take advantage of you. You look like a pretty big guy who can take care of yourself, so I'm not too worried about that, but if somebody here wants to fight you, or starts giving you shit in a hallway, whatever you do, do not fight back, just walk away. Just walk away. Or you can just call me, ain't no shame at all walking away or calling to say that somebody wants to fight you. Whatever you do, do not give any money to anybody, tell them you don't have any. I don't care what they say, how they'll pay you back, they won't. Once you give your money to somebody, you ain't never going to get it back. Now this is also Iowa, and I know everybody here claims to be Christian and all that, but they're all about as Christian as I am. Bottom line is, you're an outsider, and they'll know that about you immediately and treat you as such. Yeah, they will. One last thing. Now, I don't care what you do, but do it in your room. You know what I mean? Do it in your room, okay?"

•

Just as I had in every other city, I started the next day with a cup of coffee, a cigarette, and a walk to kick off the job hunt. While walking around downtown, I came across a Salvation Army with a handwritten Help Wanted sign taped to the front door. I asked for an application, sat down on a used sofa, and filled it out. I handed it back to the girl behind the counter. A couple days later, I received another voice mail from the day labor agency in Cheyenne, as well as one from the Salvation Army. They wanted me to come down for an interview.

•

When I showed up at 10:30 the next morning, the very first thing they had me do after signing in was take a Breathalyzer test. I passed. On the desk I saw my application. I remembered how important body language was during a job interview, so I sat on the edge of my seat, answering all of their questions: Why'd you join the military? Why do you want to work for the Salvation Army? Instead of answering, "Because I've always loved thrift stores, especially the Salvation Army," or that I wanted to know everything about thrift stores from the bottom up so that one day I could open up one of my own, or how I really valued that they were a charitable organization, I told him that I just wanted to work, and work hard, that I'd bust my ass for them. I would show up on time, and do my job without complaint.

He told me that they have a high turnover rate, and that most people just work until they receive their first paycheck, then split. Others call in sick with all sorts of excuses, like they can't come in today because their cat is sick. I told him he didn't have to worry about that with me since I didn't have a cat. He told me he liked my answers, and asked when I could start. I told him now. He explained to me that they had a part-time position available five hours a day, minimum wage, no benefits. I told him that was perfect. He asked if I knew how to get to their other Salvation Army on Euclid. I told him that I did not, that I'd just gotten into town the other day and didn't quite know my way around yet, but I could easily get directions on Google, no problem. He told me that was great and for me to show up at 10:30 the next morning for a drug test. If I passed, I'd be an employee.

I thanked him, shaking his hand. I was surprised that he didn't ask me once during the interview what had led me here to Des Moines; instead, all he asked along those lines was where I was staying, since on my application I'd written down a bogus address I just made up. When he asked me where that was, I quickly told him I was just staying there for a couple days and no longer, that I would have a new address for them.

"Oh. Where you at now?"

I tell him.

A pained look slapped across his face, like he had just stepped in dog shit.

"You're staying *there*?"

Feeling on the verge of suddenly losing this job, I told him quickly that it was just a temporary living situation until I found something else. He nodded, said that "temporary" was a good idea, and suggested for me not to stay there longer than I had to. "That's kind of a rough hotel. We deal with a lot of people who live there, since we have programs available here as well. I'd be careful."

Will do.

•

The next day, I drove the car to the Salvation Army up on Euclid. At 10:30 a.m. there were already a dozen shoppers inside. I told the girl working the counter that I was there to see Jim. She told me to follow her to the back, which I did. She moved slowly, and her walk was more of a waddle than anything else. In the back, an American flag was hung up on the wall, and there sat Jim, going over time cards. We shook hands, and he had me follow him to the bathroom to conduct the drug test. I filled a plastic cup halfway, and he handed me a plastic eyedropper, asking that I drip three drops into each hole on the little plastic drug test, which he had out on the sink. I wondered what the fuck was going on when two paper strips instantly turned color. Then a line appeared for each drug test: THC, methamphetamine, cocaine. I couldn't believe it—there were a couple nights in Omaha where I'd completely blacked out, but as far as I could remember, none of those nights had involved any illegal drugs. He then stuck his hand out and said, "Con-gratulations. Welcome to the Salvation Army!"

Standing at the position of attention, I raised my chin, and in my head I could hear the army band playing "The Stars and Stripes Forever," feeling proud. Since I was in the army now, I needed a uniform, so he told me to go to the clothing racks and pick out tan khaki pants as well as a red polo shirt; this would be my uniform. Awesome! Free clothes! All their clothing was arranged neatly, organized by gender, type, and color. It was goddamn beautiful! The efficiency and upkeep in this establishment was second to none. I walked over to where all the tan khaki pants were located, and since I'm such a stylish guy, I looked for flat-front khakis. None found. They were all pleated, which from what I understand is a fashion no-no. What-ever. I'm a size 33, and the closest thing I could find was a 38, which were not only a bit too hip-hop for me but also a couple inches too short in length, exposing my white socks. I walked over to where all the red polos were located and, hopes up that there would be a cast-off Fred Perry, began my hunt. I didn't find any, and right about the time I was giving up, close to grabbing any old red polo that fit, I nearly exclaimed, "Fuck yeah!" when I came across one that was absolutely perfect. It was a crimson red polo shirt with an embroidered Harvard University crest, with the golden word "Alumni" underneath.

Wide-eyed, I lifted it off the rack, held it up, and just stared in awe. What moron would donate his Harvard alumni shirt to Goodwill? Probably somebody who doesn't deserve to wear one, that's who. I swear, Ivy Leaguers, silver spoons, totally unappreciative of what they have, filled with a sense of entitlement. . . . Fuck this person! He or she didn't deserve to wear this polo shirt anyway, it deserves to be worn by somebody who understands and appreciates the time-honored tradition and excellence that is Harvard, and that person is *moi*. I deserve to wear it. If I had graduated from Harvard, all I would ever wear was Harvard apparel, everything that I owned would scream Harvard, even my email address, which I would spam the hell out of everyone with because it would read: colbybuzzellrules@harvard-alumni.com. Mom would be proud.

Back in the office, Jim gave my uniform an inspection—I passed. Said I looked good even. Confidently, I told him, "I know."

I was introduced to Rhonda, who I would be working with today. Rhonda has been with the Salvation Army for about eight months, and she told me that it's a great job, the days go by fast, never a dull moment. Since they like to have women work the front, men in the back, my job would be waiting around for people to show up with donated items, providing them with a tax write-off slip, then sorting all the donated items into huge cardboard boxes that sat on crates. One crate was for clothes, one for miscellaneous items, one for trash. She told me that Mondays were usually pretty busy because over the weekend people have garage sales, and on Monday they donate all the items that didn't sell. We stepped outside to have a smoke, and she lit her smoke and started to tell me that whenever you step outside for a smoke, somebody will show up to donate stuff. Which is exactly what happened. An old lady showed up in an old blue Cadillac completely filled with stuffed animals. I noticed that Rhonda didn't flick her cigarette; she just extinguished the cherry so that she could relight later, which I also did. Normally, the Salvation Army doesn't accept toys, but we took these off her hands anyway, as she was moving into a smaller living space. She told me that she had an entire room completely devoted to all her teddy bears. On her last trip, she nearly started to cry as she handed me the last box of her teddy bears.

From there, it seemed like every thirty minutes or so somebody would roll up with items to give away, and less than half wanted a tax write-off slip. Not to mention the guy who showed up with three television sets to donate—three?

I was taken aback by how high the prices were at Salvation Army; I felt that everything should have been sold for half of what they were asking. I was amazed how much stuff people buy, never use, never even touch—many items with tags still on them or still in their boxes—all ending up donated to the Salvation Army. It's like an illness. People buy stuff just to buy stuff, and to make room to buy more stuff, they donate the unused stuff.

Even the poor purchase crap they don't need. They'd come into the store, grab a cart, and I would watch them, sometimes even follow them, to see what they'd put in their cart—porcelain angels, a VHS set of the third season of *Friends*. I got the impression that the Salvation Army gave them a sense of normalcy; they could come in and afford to be consumers and purchase items, items that they either needed, felt they needed, or didn't need, just like everybody else.

•

My second day of work, I arrived a bit early, so I parked my car in the front lot and sipped coffee while waiting for ten o'clock to come around. By the front door were several plastic garbage bags filled with clothes that somebody must have dropped off overnight.

A rusty Chevy Blazer driven by an obese lady with two dirty kids in the back seat pulled up; she had one of her kids step out and grab the bags of donated clothes, then drove off.

At 9:55, a lady walked up to the front door and waited. At 10:00 a.m., the store was opened, and with my pleated khakis and red Harvard polo shirt, I started the day off by mopping the floor.

Now, usually it would take me about half an hour to mop the floor in a space like that, but I took my sweet time, since it made for fantastic people-watching.

One lady came in with three kids—two in a stroller, another in a backpack. This lady was insane; I had to follow her. Three kids! Irish triplets! One right after another! My wife can barely handle one, so while mopping, I observed her out of the corner of my eye to see how she did it. First, she went over to where all the kids' clothes were, grabbed a bunch, and then made her way over to the changing rooms in the corner. With her two kids waiting in the stroller outside the door, she went in, and when she exited, I noticed that she had a lot less kids' clothes than when she first entered. A lot less. Earlier, I'd watched an old Asian lady steal a coffee mug, casually dumping it in her purse. She saw me see her do this, and I just sort of smiled and nodded at her like *Right on old lady, fuck yeah! Don't worry, I don't care. I went to Harvard . . . it's all good.* I don't really fault these people for stealing from the Salvation Army. I think their prices are a bit steep, and don't reflect the current economic reality.

When I was done mopping, I stepped into the back. Rhonda, who was busy pricing clothes, told me to go ahead and grab the price gun and price the suitcases stacked up in the corner, placing them out on the floor when I was done. She told me the big ones should be priced at $7.99, the smaller ones $6.99. I priced them all $2.99 and put them out. Later on that day, I noticed that all of those suitcases were gone.

Harvard Business School, anyone?

•

I returned to the hotel after work, a six-pack with me. I asked the black lady I was sharing the elevator with what floor, and she told me four. Grimacing while holding her back, she told me that the morphine wasn't working and that her back was still killing her.

"Really?"

"Yup. Twenty milligrams. I got some methadone, too, but that won't do anything."

Once all the beers were drained, I found myself bored with drinking in my room. After pacing for a bit, I decided to go out and do something else.

I ordered a shot and a beer at the bar next door. While thinking long and hard about how there's got to be more to life than drinking in your room every night, I heard a voice ask me when I got back. I came to, looked over, black guy about my age also drinking by himself. His question took me off guard, so I asked what he meant by that, and he repeated himself, this time adding, "When'd you get back from the war?"

I had no article of clothing on me as evidence that I was ever in the military, so I asked, "How'd you know? Were you in the military?"

He shook his head, told me no, and while holding onto his pint glass told me, "You can just tell."

Wow. Time for a makeover. Did I really look that depressing? I'd honestly lost track of how many years it had been since I'd come back from deployment, and so far it had all been a blur. I knew deep down inside I was wasting the best years of my life by opting to drink my way through them, but I just didn't know what else to do. What was there to do? Something needed to happen to get me out of this routine, I just wasn't sure what that was yet.

I left the bar. Every town along I-80 seems to have railroad track running parallel to it, and this one was no exception. While wandering around semi-drunk, I came across a couple scruffy-looking guys with backpacks and sleeping bags who were looking to jump on a train. Mid-twenties. They were looking for a train with a floorboard, and I asked them where they were headed off to; they told me Kansas City. One of the train hoppers had green hair and a weight problem. When I asked him why he was jumping a train, he told me that there's nothing in Des Moines: "It sucks here and my parents hate me, so fuck them, I'm leaving." Which is what he did.

I watched them jump on a train and, with no gesture of a good-bye, leave.

I then thought about my own life. Another train going in the opposite direction was pulling up. I had a vision of jumping in front of it. Then it slowly came to a halt.

My thoughts were drunk, and either I could jump on this train and run away forever and abandon everything—this book, the life I had, and all my worldly possessions, all of it—or I could . . .

I jumped on. Minutes later, it started to move. It felt like freedom.

I didn't go far, just over the river, and once on the other side of the bridge, I jumped off before it could pick up speed. I made my way over to a bar. When the bartender asked me where I was from, I told him, and that I had hopped a train to get here, which was partially true. He gave me a free shot. I thanked him with a tip.

I thought long and hard about what I should do, where I should go, how I could get to the goddamn climax. Then I got an idea. I ordered another round, got drunk, blacked out, and don't remember much. I slept through my alarm clock, which meant I didn't show up to work, which meant I lost my job. Which meant I had a drinking problem.

I had to leave.

•

Checkout was at noon, I was forty-five minutes late, and I couldn't find my car keys. Finally, I found them stashed away in a coat pocket. I grabbed my shit and left. When I stepped into the elevator down the hall, as his back was turned to me, I saw that the guy I was sharing the ride with had a fifth of vodka peeking out of his back pocket. I'd seen him before hanging out both inside and out of the hotel, and I was sure he'd seen me doing the same, but this time I looked different. This time I had all my personal belongings with me, and he looked over at me, up and down, taking notice that I was carrying my military duffel bag, backpack, and sleeping bag—which I used to keep me warm at night, since the room had no goddamn heating— and I could smell the alcohol on his breath as he asked me if I was leaving. I told him that I was, and when he asked me where to, I told him Detroit. Intrigued, he opened his eyes up a bit and kind of shifted his body toward mine and asked, "What for?"

"Just cuz."

So far, whenever I've told somebody that I'm traveling "just cuz," they get suspicious and think I'm trafficking in drugs or running from the law, something screwy like that . . . though there was this one smart lady, a bartender working a dive over by the train tracks in Laramie, Wyoming, who, when she discovered that I was driving by myself across the country, quickly said, "Let me guess, there's a woman involved."

"Nope," I quickly lied.

"You're going there just because?" the guy in the elevator asked. "To Detroit? For no reason at all?"

Shaking his head, thinking, he stopped, and I saw a smile about to crack on his face. By now we were passing the second floor.

He asked, "What are you, like a vagabond or something?"

"Naw. Not really. Just doing the whole Kerouac thing, that's all."

"What?"

"Long story."

The elevator doors opened up, and the guy just kind of stood there in bewilderment, slightly shaking his head. Then he snapped out of it, put his fist out so that we could hit fists together, and wished me luck. I thanked him as he went his way, and I went mine.

The guy working the desk at the hotel was an older gentleman, and didn't say much. Behind him on the wall were a series of wooden slots for the mail coming in for the people who lived in the building. Most were empty. The man had white hair and a series of old sun-faded prison-style tattoos up and down both arms. They were so old that I couldn't really tell what they were anymore, and while he fished my $25 deposit for the week, and my $5 deposit for the key, out of the old school register, I looked over at the back table, where a guy was passed out, head down on the table. Next to his head was a stack of day-old bread for the people who live here. I'd been living off that bread since landing at the hotel, and I thought to myself how sick I was of that bread. Too many carbs. I got my money and split. After passing by all the bail-bond businesses next door, I made my way over to my mistress.

When I got inside, I saw that there was a piece of paper underneath one of my windshield wipers. The note stated that I was illegally parked, that the parking space I was in was reserved for the people living in the condos next door, and that if I did it again, they'd have me towed. I looked up at the condo and frowned. It looked like it was designed by somebody who spent way too much time as a color-blind child playing with square Legos, and nothing else. I crumpled up the note and threw it into the pile of other garbage down on the floorboard of the passenger side. I lit up a smoke and made my way over to the freeway, glad to be leaving Des Moines and on to somewhere else. When I pulled onto the freeway heading east, for the very first time on this journey, I made my way over to the fast lane and stayed there.

CHAPTER ELEVEN

Detroit

"There is no substitute for Victory."

GENERAL ÐOUGLAS MACARTHUR

June 6, 1944, the largest amphibious assault ever in the history of warfare took place on the beaches of Normandy, France. While driving lockjawed and staring straight ahead, sights on Detroit, I envisioned myself as an E-4 infantryman, my 2nd ID combat patch on my right shoulder, locked and loaded, riding on the back of a landing craft headed straight toward Omaha Beach. It was about a ten-hour drive from Des Moines, which meant I'd get there sometime in the middle of the night, which should be fun.

•

The term *postapocalyptic* is often used when referring to Detroit. After one radiator, two oil changes, three generators, four balding tires, and more than four and a half thousand miles on an engine built during the Johnson administration, I was there.

It didn't take me long at all to realize that Detroit was the perfect city to be alone, since there was hardly anybody else here, which instantly put me in a blissfully soulful mood. If only my car stereo worked so that I could listen to "South of Heaven" by Slayer—the opening would have been the perfect soundtrack as I crept into the concrete ghost town.

"Before you see the light you must die!"

Navigating my vehicle through the dark sea of urban decay, I decided it was time to park, dismount, and patrol the area on foot. I turned into a parking garage. A black guy wearing a hat and yellow jacket was working the booth, and kind of lit up when he saw me pull up to grab a ticket. He pulled open his booth window, eyed my ride enviously, asked me what year it was, and even guessed '64.

"You are correct," I told him.

"How much you pay for that?"

"More than what I wanted to but a little less than I expected."

"California car?"

"Yup. Drove it all the way here."

"You drove all the way here from California?"

"Fuck, yeah. Been on the road for a while now, and um, yup, now I'm here."

"What you got going here in Detroit?"

"I don't know yet. What's there to do here?"

He told me of a couple nearby bars and restaurants that were in walking distance, which of course went in one ear and out the other, since you can find those in any city no problem. When I asked him if he was from here, he told me no, originally he's from Chicago, but he'd lived here for the last couple of years now. When I asked how he ended up here, he said, "Wife and kids," and "You know how it is."

Actually, I don't know how it is. I pretended I wasn't freaking out as it occurred to me that my life could also change in that same way.

"Is it safe for me to walk around here at night?"

He shook his head casually and simply told me, "You know how it is. The world is a ghetto."

Was that a rap song, lyric, or the name of a Nas album? Not sure.

"What do you mean?"

He then broke it down for me: it was the same in Detroit as anywhere else, and as long as I didn't go around acting a fool and get caught up in shit that I shouldn't be involved in, I'd be all right.

Sounds like prison.

He told me that he's lived all over during his lifetime. "I've even lived down in the South for a bit, and in my life I've been the only black on the block twice, and Detroit is just like anywhere else, man. As long as you do yo' shit, don't bother nobody, don't get caught up in nobody else's business, then you be all right. Just do your thang, you know? Be a loner, don't be gettin' stoned with nobody, and you be all right. Detroit ain't that bad, it really ain't, nope."

I thanked him, and before I pulled into the garage, he told me one other thing. "And don't be going around here badmouthing Detroit. People here, they don't like that. They love their city, don't know what that is, but they do and they don't like it when other people come up in here and badmouth it. They got a lot a pride here in they city."

I parked the Caliente up on one of the top levels and stepped out of the parking garage. I saw that there was a chain-link fence all around the building across the street, which was heavily grafittied from top to bottom. Hung on the fence was a warning sign: "Demolition Work in Progress."

Instead of destroying it, why don't they restore it?

Next to the condemned building was a name-brand hotel. As with Walmart, I try to avoid those, but as with Walmart, sometimes you don't have much of a choice in the matter. Since it was getting kind of late, I decided to just check that out instead of driving all over the place all night looking for a place to crash.

A couple of businessmen wearing suits and ties walked out of the hotel lobby; I did a double take as I made my way past them. I asked the lady working the desk how much for a night. She told me the walk-in rate is $110. I nearly fainted. Leaning with my arm resting on the counter, I thought, Goddamn, that's way over my budget for a night in this town. With the exception of Motel 6, I'd noticed that the hotels with brand names and commercials on the tube went anywhere from $70 to $150 a night, no matter where they were. Shit added up after a while.

That's partially why I'd been frequenting the down-and-out weekly and monthly hotels that run about eighty to a hundred a week. Some have toilets and showers in the room, some don't, some have hot water, some don't, most are filled with people living off GA (government assistance, aka your tax dollars at work), just staying in their rooms waiting for the day to end, loners who have lived there for years and who spend most of their time trying to drink themselves to death. Every single one of these hotels has one or two residents who insist on borrowing money from you and promises to God that they'll pay you back. Some will even knock on your door at three in the morning, asking you for a couple bucks or a cigarette. These establishments aren't to be found anywhere online, which is kind of refreshing, since the mysteries of the entire world are now solved with a few clicks. Not these gems. You must seek them out.

There are several ways you can find these hotels. You can ask any police officer where the bad part of town is located and just start walking in that direction. Or ask any homeless-looking person on the street, and ten times out of ten they'll point you in the right direction as well as ask you for some spare change. Adding helpfully, "I wouldn't really stay there if I were you. People die there all the time."

Since it was getting late, and I'd rather explore than waste my time looking around all night for a motel, I decided to just check into the Holiday Inn Express. But first I needed to get this lady to lower the price somehow. From experience I've found that hotels are kind of like antique stores; the price that they initially give you isn't necessarily the price that you'll pay. So with a pained face I asked her if that was the best she could do. She told me that it was, and when I asked her if she knew of any others in the neighborhood that were more reasonably priced, she then told me that she could do $79 for a night. Still way over my budget, but since it was late, I told her she had herself a deal.

•

I'd now gotten my wish, I was all alone. In Detroit of all places, all by myself, at night, lost, unarmed, half a pack

of smokes left, hadn't shaved in a week and I couldn't remember the last time I did laundry. I guess the look that I
unintentionally had right then, with the beanie, thrashed
Cons, thrashed dark gray nonpleated khakis, filthy gray
socks that used to be white, thrashed flannel—buttoned up
all the way, since I'm from the West Coast—and thrashed
hooded sweatshirt, I guess this look would be considered
homeless or jobless chic, and I think I have this look down,
because many times on this trip people I came across on
the street would ask me if I was homeless and recommend
places for me to eat. I've gotten plenty of free meals thanks
to this look, mostly at churches. And people will also tell
me where all the shelters are located. But it's more than the
clothes. I think you also have to walk around with this defeated appearance as well, which I've noticed many people
here have, too.

After dropping off my shit in my room, I hit the streets
with nothing but my military-issue digital camo backpack
and a camera around my neck.

As I walked around downtown Detroit, I noticed that
there was not a whole heck of a lot of foot traffic, and most of
the buildings were boarded up, empty, totally dark, nearly
all with FOR SALE and/or FOR LEASE signs, many with fore-
closure notices stapled to the door. I came upon a historic
plaque on the side of a building. It stated that the building was the "Birthplace of the Ford Automobile." I looked
in the lobby. A black guy wearing a security uniform was
working behind the desk; leaning back in his seat, he appeared bored. I walked around the building and saw that
on the side there had once been a theater of some sort, but

now it was all fenced off and dilapidated and seemed to have been turned into some kind of parking structure.

I wanted to check it out, legally, so I went inside and asked the black guy if I could please have his permission to do so. His expression didn't change one bit as he denied my request with a simple "No."

Okay, I could see that I'd have to use some finesse here, so I asked him if this was fairly common, people like me just walking in and asking if they could check it out. He releases a yawn. "Yes," he manages.

Getting him to talk was like pulling teeth, so I decided to go ahead and ask: About how many of those people, would you say, that come in and ask if they can have your permission get your permission?

Eyelids remaining at half-mast, he told me that he denied nine out of ten requests. Nine out of ten is not bad—it's better than ten out of ten—and when I asked him what exactly I had to do to be in that lucky 10 percent, he told me that I had to be either filming a movie or a professional photographer, both of which I'm not.

I guessed I was shit out of luck then, so I thanked him for his time, and as I was about to exit so that I could just physically hop the fence myself to sneak a peek, he asked me where I'm from, so I told him, and that I'd just got here, and we got to talking. I asked how safe it was for me to walk around here, and he told me that I was fine, that no random crimes happened here really, most of the crimes that went on involved both parties knowing each other. He came to life, sort of, and worked to make a point. "It's not that bad here," he said. I again thanked him for his time, and this time as I was about to leave he released a sigh, picked up his keys off the desk, got up from his chair, and told me to follow him. Awesome. I followed, and he guided me up a flight of stairs and opened up a door for me. "You have ten minutes and ten minutes only," he said.

I stepped in, with both eyes wide open taking in as much as I can, and he asked me what I thought. I took it in for a couple seconds. "It's beautiful," I said.

"Ten minutes," he said. "That's all you got." He turned around and walked away, leaving me in there all by myself. I was in shock, and couldn't fucking believe that I was having a near religious experience inside a fucking parking garage. I then started going crazy with the camera.

The only car parked there was a black late-model Mercedes. It sat there all by itself, surrounded by the walls, the moldings, the faded colors, the decay, all of it beautiful. At least they turned this structure into a parking garage and didn't tear it down, I thought. But at the same time I wondered why we don't build theaters like this anymore.

Thanking the security guy, I headed toward an area several blocks away where I had seen a lot of cars were parked. I looked down at my watch, and wondered why I hadn't been mugged or robbed yet. After walking across several empty lots, I stopped at a street corner. Several Mercedes, a Hummer, a Lexus, late-model SUVs with expensive rims were parked right there at Park Avenue and West Montcalm Street, sandwiched between two bars. I looked into the windows at one of the bars, a place called Centaur, and was stunned to see an extremely upscale joint—art deco interior, a martini bar, and everybody inside dressed up

like they were on their way to the theater, or headed to a
ball game at Comerica Park, where the Tigers play. There
wasn't much life along these blocks, but here they were.
The bar was located on the first floor of a restored building; the floors above it looked like high-end lofts. I crossed
the street heading over to the bar on the other corner, the
Town Pump. Peering into the windows I saw all the business casual attire. Everyone looked as if they had money,
and were having a great time, too. It all seemed to be for
my benefit, like actors staging a fabulous dinner party on a
barren Beckett landscape; as soon as I left, they'd break set
and go home to the suburbs. I took a step back and looked
up at the building. This one towered many stories, and it
was called the Park Avenue Hotel. When I peeked in the
lobby, it looked like one of those hotels that cater to those
in the lower tax brackets, featuring weekly and monthly
rates.

I walked inside.

•

The lobby interior of the Park Avenue Hotel was old-school
Italian Renaissance. A black guy was silently smoking a
cigarette and listening to jazz, slowly dragging behind the
old wooden lobby desk, with wooden mail slots on the wall
behind him. He unenthusiastically buzzed me in through
the heavy steel gate. I crept in and asked the guy if they
had any rooms available and if they had weekly rates, since
after my visit with my buddy Callahan I'd need a place to
stay in Detroit. He told me that they did have weekly rates,
but right now they were all booked up. This, I thought,
was amazing. I'd never encountered this before; every SRO

(single room occupancy) hotel I'd ever been to had a vacancy. He told me to come back in a couple of days, and something might have opened up. I thanked him, and before leaving, I noticed that right there on the corner of the desk was a huge stack of the *Times Literary Supplement*, *New York Times*, *Wall Street Journal*, and *Financial Times*, as well as a couple back issues of the *Economist*. Interesting. I asked him who those belonged to, he told me the owner. I told him I'd be back and stepped outside, wondering what to do next. I took a glance over to my left, across the freeway, and noticed that the area over there was the complete opposite to the one I was standing in the middle of. It screamed, "Stay away!" The street lights over there didn't seem to shine as bright, and there were two towering abandoned hotel buildings surrounded by vacant lots, a couple beat cab companies, a divey-looking liquor store, a handful of abandoned and boarded-up buildings, a couple semi-burned-down, perfect-for-crack houses, and one or two people just idling on dark street corners, hooded sweatshirts with the hood up, just standing there, and one or two people just walking slowly, like *Night of the Living Dead*, one step at a time, slowly, slowly, over a graveyard, their heads down. Lost.

•

The game was on the television when I walked into the bar. An angry old-timer was telling a couple other barflies all about how it's a goddamn ripoff to purchase season tickets and why in the world should he do that, spending a couple hundred dollars for seats when he can just sit in a bar a couple blocks away and watch the games for free, as well as the drinks at the bar are way cheaper than the ones they sell at the stadium. He had a point; why do anything at all when it's cheaper not to do it, or to do it at home, in a bar, or on the computer?

I asked the bartender—who, I could tell by his tattoos, listened to hardcore punk bands—if he knew of any good weekly and monthly hotels. He actually lived at one, and after he told me where it was located, we got to talking about Detroit and he told me that a lot of films get made here now. "Yeah, Drew Barrymore has done two movies here already because they got a new tax break thing if you film in Michigan, and they're doing a lot of films here. Quite a few movies are going to be filmed here, *Gran Torino* was also filmed here—"

"They shot *Gran Torino* here?"

"Yeah, they shot that, and now they're shooting the new *Red Dawn* downtown, and they're doing another movie here that's about the Irish gangs in Cleveland but they're using this neighborhood because it's more run-down and fucked up than Cleveland is—now that they kind of cleaned Cleveland up a lot."

A regular down at the end of the bar heard this and blurted out, "Amen to Cleveland!"

I raised my beer to that, and just then a white guy with dreadlocks walked in. He and the bartender were good friends, and the bartender introduced him to me. A musician, he was actually in a Misfits cover band. He also worked on the assembly line at Ford, putting Ford Focuses together. He told me he'd got off work early tonight because they'd run out of parts to assemble, so they let everybody go halfway through their shift. I asked if that happened a lot, and he told me not all the time, but it happened, and when it did, the funny thing was that all the guys would go directly to the bars, especially the married guys, they'd go to the bars and wouldn't tell their wives that they got released early from work, because if they did their wives would be like get your ass home, and the females, what they'd do was go straight to the casinos, and they'd do the same thing, they wouldn't tell their husbands that they'd got off work early, they'd just go straight to the casino and then come home afterward like they just got off work. Basically what he told me was what auto industry people do when they're told to go home, not working, or out of a job.

Since he was in a Misfits cover band and into punk, we talked music for a while, and later on, after he left, I found myself sitting down next to an old black guy. Casually sipping on his beer, he told me that he'd lived in Detroit since 1950.

"I came from out of the Midwest because there was no work out there, and so I came here and I got a job about eight hours after I got off the bus. Back in the fifties you could get hired in the morning, work a day, quit the next morning, and have another job by noon the next day."

After taking a slow swig from his beer, he said, "Those days are over."

He told me that he'd never seen Detroit as bad as it was now; this was the worst he'd seen it.

"Call it what you want to call it, but it's a depression here in Detroit. You see we put all our effort into the auto industry, and when the auto industry fails, then where do you go? We put all our eggs into one basket. They could have diversified years ago, but they didn't. Young people don't know what a depression is. People were jumping out of their windows back then because they got broke and lost all their money. But there was a lot of people who survived. Right now, I don't know how many people are jumping out of windows, but there is a survival situation going on. You should read about it. The rest of America is beginning to feel what we felt nine months ago."

I then left this bar to walk over to another one down the street. Ordered a couple beers and shots of whiskey at a bar called AFB, which as you could have probably figured out on your own means "Another Fucking Bar." Their slogan was: "Exactly what Detroit needs." Kind of a fancy joint inside, a bit upscale—keep in mind that's upscale by my standards. A patron next to me at the bar told me that it was once a popular punk venue before they cleaned it up. After that I set off to walk around and explore, semi-drunk, since I hadn't eaten all day. I started taking photos of dark streets and alleys, empty lots, garbage on the streets, houses boarded up. Some halfway burned-down parts of the area felt, especially at night, as if nobody lived there at all and I was the only person left on earth. I walked over to two tall old buildings that looked like they had both been hotels at one time and stood there, wondering what had happened to them. I took pictures. They looked as if they'd been vacant for years; one was called the Harbor Lights Center, and the other the Hotel Eddy Stone. Some clever jokester had hung up on the Eddy Stone a huge MOVE IN NOW! banner followed by a phone number to call.

This area was totally dead—way more dead than downtown—and in a lot of ways reminded me of my neighborhood back home, the Tenderloin district. There we have roughly four to six crackheads along every street, whereas here there were maybe only one or two crackheads every three or four city blocks. This is a statistic of civic comparison that you never see in the brochures. Colby Buzzell: travel writer.

With my black beanie pulled down almost over my eyes, I was wondering where in the hell everybody was when I came across two guys smoking outside a structure that looked operational. They were both staring at me as I walked over to them. An American flag was sticking up from the building they were standing in front of, so I asked the two of them what the place was exactly, and they told me that it was a shelter for veterans.

One of them immediately asked me if I was a vet, since I was wearing my backpack. "You homeless?" he asked. I told him that I was kind of living out of my car right now— which was partially true; I had spent many a night sleeping in the Caliente—but I was planning to stay at an army buddy's place for a couple days up in Troy, and then after that I'd be back. He told me that I should stay here when I came back, and that they had a good bunch of guys living here. It was warm, and they served three meals a day. He then asked what I was doing here—more specifically, in the location where I was now standing—and I told them just checking out, walking around, taking pictures, that kind of stuff. He advised me not to be walking around in this area with a camera around my neck because the people here would look at that as ten crack rocks and gank me for it. I looked around, not seeing anybody, and asked him if this was a bad neighborhood. The one guy furrowed his brows and curiously asked me, "Do you know where you are?"

I had a couple shots of whiskey running through my veins, and that one GN'R song where Axl poses that very same question started playing in my head. He informed me that I'm in the murder capital of the state of Michigan, and not only that, "You're in the Cass Corridor."

I told him that I'd never heard of it, though it did sound kind of tough, and he advised me that I really shouldn't be walking around here late at night all by myself, especially with a camera around my neck, and since I was a vet, he told me that I should stay at the shelter for the night, that if I did I'd be safe. "Nobody fucks with us here," he proudly told me. "One time one of our guys got fucked with, and we had three teams of guys go out with baseball bats, and ever since then nobody messes with us."

I thanked them for their time and told them that I'd check it out in a couple days, after I visit my friend from the army up in Troy for a couple days. They wished me luck and again told me to be careful. I thanked them.

•

Hung over, the next morning I called the front desk and told them that I'd be a bit late checking out, since I was having difficulty locating my wallet. I thought I might have lost it in the bar or on my way back to my room or something like that. They said that was fine, and forty-five minutes later I found it hiding tangled in a bed sheet.

Heading to the elevator, I thought back to the night

before, about how the neighborhood was rumored to be rough despite the fact that it's relatively close to Wayne State University. I've lived in areas on the cusp of gentrification, I guess contributing to it—for better or worse—but this didn't feel the same; the random hipster in a sea of dilapidated buildings, but not the same. On my way down I noticed that this hotel didn't have a thirteenth floor, and when I finally made my way to checkout, a band on tour looked like they were checking out at the same time and moving on to the next city. Lucky bastards. They at least knew where they were going next. While waiting for my receipt, I asked the guy working the front desk if it was hard to find a job here. He told me no, as long as you're willing to work for whatever pay, which is the exact answer I've been getting all across the country. He then told me that just this morning, while installing cable at his new apartment, the Comcast guy tried to recruit him, and I should just go online and apply if I was looking for work. Cable guy in Detroit, that could be interesting. So I asked if it was bad here, and he released a laugh and told me that he was actually late to work this morning because some idiot decided to go up and down deflating all the tires of every single car parked on his street.

•

Over by the freeway was a huge old cement building painted light blue, selling nothing but used and rare books. It was like the Powell's Books of Detroit; you could spend hours if not days inside and not be bored. It'll be a sad day indeed when bookstores no longer exist. So I went to check it out while it still stood.

I instantly got absorbed in the vision of old Detroit offered by the store's vast collection of old linen postcards. Detroit looks nowhere near the same now. Those two hotels I'd looked at in the Cass Corridor the night before were once beautiful, with retail spaces on their bottom floors, and these Technicolor portraits of yesteryear were plainly of a different city altogether, a city of state-of-the-art architecture and young men in a hurry. Most of the cards had two or three cursive sentences on the back, saying things like, "Dear folks, we are in Detroit and I am working at my trade. Nice weather for this time of year. All are well. Mom has sold the chickens, Love to all." That one was mailed November 25, 1910.

Another one depicted "The Heart of Detroit by Moonlight," and on back in an elegant cursive you just don't find anymore, it read: "Everything is okay except I don't have a job yet. Things are pretty slow all around here. Most of the shops are laying men off right and left, but look for it to pick up soon. I hope so. Rabbit season has been in for 3 weeks but haven't gone yet. Well, so long." The ink stamp said that it was mailed from Detroit on November 6, 1937, at 4:30 p.m.

Another had a gorgeous image of Capital Square Park from that same era, which looks nothing like that now; all the vegetation in the square is gone, and half the buildings around it are gone as well. The card read, "I am so busy I can hardly find time to write. Wages are low in Detroit. One has a hard time to pay for their board and room. Hope you will like these postcards of Detroit. Will send more soon."

While I was lost in old Detroit, a young employee who looked like an artist came by and told a coworker that a kid just came in asking if they had any books on how to make an IED. I remember one time back in high school I was once called down to the principal's office for doing a book report on *The Anarchist Cookbook*, and since it was pre-Columbine and pre-Osama when I wrote it, all that happened was my parents received yet another phone call from the school administration telling them how much of a fuckup I was. "Hey," I asked the clerk, "do you sell *The Anarchist Cookbook*?" She told me no, and that when she first started working here twenty-three years ago, she thought the book was just recipes that were staples of the anarchist diet, but then later on she found out that it was instructions for how to make bombs. She told me that people didn't really ask for that book too much now, maybe partly because you could find all those recipes online now.

I then asked her if she had the WPA book that was done on Michigan. The Works Progress Administration was a New Deal thing that Roosevelt did. Unlike chain mega bookstore employees who ask you, "Who wrote that?" when you ask if they have a copy of *Men Without Women*, and then ask you how you spell Hemingway, this lady knew exactly what I was talking about. She told me that they did actually have a copy, behind the counter, and handed it to me to check out—green cloth hardcover, no dust jacket but a cool deco-style imprint on the front of an automobile and a factory behind it, the sun beaming down on both. I opened it up, saw that they were asking $35 for it, as is, and that it was first published in 1941. I started flipping through all the pages. The section on Detroit began, "A visitor may spend weeks in Detroit without receiving the impression that he is in a city of more than 1,500,000 inhabitants."

Seventy years later, Detroit's now at 900,000, and dropping like a rock. I told the bookstore lady I'd take it.

CHAPTER TWELVE

The End

*"We are what we pretend to be, so we must be
careful about what we pretend to be."*

KURT VONNEGUT,
Mother Night

While I spent the day walking aimlessly around Detroit
taking pictures, my sister sent me a text informing me that
our father had decided that he was going to sell the house
that we all grew up in. I didn't respond because I didn't
know what to say or think of that, though I saw it coming
and don't blame my father at all.

Knowing that the house I grew up in will no longer
be there when I get back made me want to drink in a bar.
All the memories—Christmas, Thanksgiving, etc.—that
we shared at that house would be no longer. In a way, I
was homeless now. Equally important, that house had
also been the place where I always ended up whenever I
hit rock bottom and needed a place to stay for a while as I
tried once again to get back on my feet. I always knew that
it would be there. Yes, as I got older the welcome arms of
home weren't as welcoming. There was never a "Welcome
Home, Colby!" banner strung across the living room when

I moved back in. But still, it was there for me in case of an emergency. My mother lived and died in that house. All of a sudden I felt that I was about to jump out of a plane behind enemy lines without a parachute.

My phone started to vibrate; it was Callahan. He said he was out of class and wanted to hang out. I was near downtown, and my watch told me it was close to five. When I asked him how bad traffic would be at this time of day, he told me not to worry. "You'll be fine. Nobody's working anymore, so there's not as much traffic."

•

Before leaving I stopped back inside a dive bar. A sign posted outside the bar advertised free wireless, and I needed to pull up directions to Callahan's place, so I stepped inside, ordered a pack of smokes from the bartender, tipped her a dollar, made my way to a corner table, and pulled out my laptop. While I was looking up directions, a tall old black guy with a white apron around his waist walked slowly over to me and silently placed a tray of onion rings on my table. When I told him, "I'm sorry, I didn't order anything," he said in this really deep voice, perhaps the deepest voice I've ever heard, "I know." And then slowly he turned around and walked away.

When I pulled my car out of the parking garage, the same guy was working. I handed him my ticket, and he told me that would be $18.00. Jesus Christ. No wonder nobody went downtown anymore. As I was handing him the money, he asked me what I thought of Detroit. I told him that except that they charged way too much for parking, I liked Detroit a lot, actually. While getting my change ready, he told me that he wasn't surprised to hear that. He explained that the world makes it out to be such a bad city because "Detroit is a dark city. A lot of us blacks live here, and some people don't like that, that's why they be sayin' what they be sayin'."

Callahan lives north of Eight Mile out in the 'burbs, past Sixteen Mile Road up in Troy, which is about a good half hour drive north of downtown Detroit. He and his girlfriend live at her parents' house; both are in school, his girlfriend studying hard to be a nurse.

After he left the army, Callahan moved with another buddy of ours, Sergeant Todd Vance, down to San Diego. When I used to live in Los Angeles I'd go down there every now and then to hang out with them. Callahan was having difficulty finding work, and one day he'd packed up all his belongings in the back of his pickup truck and driven straight through to Michigan, where he has family. He's lived there ever since.

The room I was sleeping in was down in the basement, which had been converted into a full bar with bar stools, neon beer signs, mirrors, TV, liquor, the works. After dropping off my stuff we stepped outside for a smoke, and while we caught up, Callahan said hello to the girl standing and smoking outside the house across the street. She was about my age—early thirties. It was cold out, and I know some people don't like to smoke in their own house, so I didn't really think much of it until I looked at all the driveways on the street. The house across the street had four cars parked outside it, the one to the right of it, six, the one next door, four, and so on. I asked Callahan about the girl smoking across the way, and he told me that she also was back living at her parents' house.

We decided to hit the bars that evening, and on the way Callahan told me that he was a student right now, living off the GI Bill, and that they'd recently raised GI benefits so that he got slightly more now every month than he did before. He worked one day a week as a bar back for tips, and the tips that he made working Friday nights, always close to $100, pretty much lasted him for the week, "My gas tank is always on red, but I've got enough to live on right now."

When I asked what his plans were after school, he told me that he didn't know yet, he might try and get a job at the VA hospital working with other veterans, or he might continue going to school and take out student loans once his GI Bill money dried up. I strongly advised him against doing this because the one thing about student loans is that it's not really "free money," like a lot of people think it is. You have to pay that all back, along with the lovely interest they throw on top of it, and I know many educated people back home who are totally fucked because they took out these huge student loans, graduated, couldn't find a job, and are now totally poor because all of the money they are now making in their restaurant server jobs goes straight to paying back all their student loans. The days of "Well, I'll take out loans to go to school, and when I graduate I'll get a job in that field making the lavish salary I require" are gone. Or maybe I'm just rationalizing the fact that I forgot to go to college, and so had no use for student loans. I will have to think about this.

Callahan said that most of the people that he knew were either in school, living off student loans, or on unemployment. While driving around looking for a parking spot, I noticed that we were passing by a lot of hair salons, and that these hair salons were all packed with people, and that all the people were getting their hair done, and that they were all getting their hair done in the same exact hairstyle as each other, and all the girls in Orange County, in New York, in Austin, in Kalamazoo, and in Poughkeepsie, too.

At the bar everybody had a beer in hand and was drinking heavily. One guy at the end of the bar had a textbook out, reading while drinking, and a lot of people were doing multiple shots of hard liquor. I looked over at the guy sitting next to me at the bar. The sleeves on his shirt had been physically removed, and he was easily about four hundred pounds. He ordered another pitcher of beer, and he was drinking out of it as if it was a pint glass. I asked him if he was unemployed, and he told me that he was, actually. He'd been driving trucks, got laid off several months ago, and was living off unemployment.

Callahan was sitting at the bar to my right, and I pointed this out to him. He told me, "I told you." A guy then came between us to order a drink—white guy, early thirties, frosted tips, Red Wings hockey jersey, silver chain around his neck—and I asked him if he was working. He told me that he was at the GM plant and, with no worry or concern in his voice whatsoever, that he'd be getting laid off next month. "You nervous?" I asked him.

He shrugged. "Not at all." He'd been laid off four times

in the last nine years, and he said it was no big deal, that's just how it was when you worked in the auto industry. He said he'd find something, even if it was minimum wage, and he picked up his drink and walked off. Everybody in this bar was getting completely trashed, drinking nonstop like it was one big unemployment party. Didn't these people know how fucked they were? They all had a "This too shall pass" attitude about their lives and our current economic situation, and when Callahan's friends started showing up at the bar, I found out that all of them—*all of them*—were living back at home and unemployed or going back to school.

At the bar one of Callahan's friends started asking me about the book that I was working on. He asked me what I thought of the country so far, and since I had a couple drinks in me, I asked him if he'd ever been inside a Walmart. I was starting to think that if Kerouac were alive today, he'd probably go to China to write *On the Road.*

Callahan's friend then asked me where I was headed after Detroit. I told him, "I don't know yet. I don't know what city I'm off to next until I get there. . . ." For some reason I paused for a second, knowing that there was more to this than what I just said. "I don't know why this is, yet, but I'm actually thinking about ending it here in Detroit."

"Most people do," he says.

Smile.

•

The next morning when I woke up, I saw that I was out of smokes, so I took off to the gas station on foot to restock.

On my walk back to Callahan's I came across a yard sale, a one-story located on a busy street with the garage open and all sorts of items out for sale. They even had a couple moped scooters for sale, the kind that I'd seen a lot of the Academy of Art kids like to ride around on back home, one of which had a price tag of $600. When the guy came out, a white guy about retirement age, I asked him about the moped, wondering if a big guy like me—six-one, two hundred or so pounds, who could easily bench-press 275 prior to this road trip—could ride on one of those things. He told me yeah, no prob. "Gets eighty miles to the gallon," he said, and when he told me that he could sell me one for $400 but not less, I asked him why he was selling all his stuff. He was moving, he said; he had purchased a place in the South. I then told him that I was from California, had just gotten here the other day, was staying at a friend's place around the corner for now, and that I liked the scooter a lot and that it would be perfect for what I was going to do. I told him that I could cover a lot more ground and navigate my way up, down, and around downtown Detroit a hell of a lot better on a moped than on foot, and when I told him this, his whole attitude shifted and he didn't want to sell it to me anymore.

"You want to drive around downtown Detroit on this thing?"

"Yeah. It's perfect."

"I've worked in downtown Detroit for thirty years building bridges, and I would never, ever, go down there unless I had a firearm on me. Do you own a firearm?"

"No."

He then shook his head and lost all interest in me.

•

When I walked into the lobby of the Park Avenue Hotel, an older white lady was leaning against the lobby desk, talking to the black guy working behind it. I asked if they had any rooms available, and what they cost. The lady told me that they had one, and she sized me up and asked how much I could afford to pay for it. I politely told her that I didn't want to offend her by suggesting a low amount, and that I'd pay the amount that they were asking for it as long as it was reasonable. She then asked if I was employed and what I did for work, since they also only rent out to people who have jobs. This was a first. Most of the places that I'd stayed at didn't care as long as you could pay the rent.

Be the person you want to be.

With a straight face I told her that I was a writer. Yes, a writer from California who was just traveling across the country doing what writers do, working hard on a book, and long story short, here I was in Detroit.

While I stood frozen in fear, not quite sure if she'd believe me, not quite sure if I believed me, she asked, "You're a writer?"

"I don't believe it either, but yeah, I guess I am."

She warmed up to me a bit and asked where I'd been, and after I listed off all the cities and states I'd passed through on my way here, she got back to work and asked how much I'd paid for the last place I was staying. I was paying ninety a week at that last place back in Des Moines, and seeing the sign on the counter that indicated a hundred a week, I told her that I'd been paying eighty in hopes that she'd meet me halfway. She shook her head and told me that she couldn't do eighty, that was way too low, but she could do a hundred a week. Doing the math in my head, I figured out that it'd be four hundred for a month, which ain't too bad, so I started reaching for my wallet.

"Cool. I'll take it."

"Don't you want to see the room?"

"Oh, yeah, sure."

She grabbed the keys and took me up to the third floor. She was wearing jeans, a floral-patterned blouse, hair pulled back like she was ready to work. I got the impression that she was a very kind lady as well as a very tough one, and while we waited for the elevator to come down she informed me that she and her husband managed this building as well as the building next door, and then she looked at me. "What are you?" she asked. I tell her that I'm half Korean and half white. She then very proudly told me that she was Dutch, which explained her thick accent, and that where she was from they don't look at color like they do here, and that she didn't discriminate, and more importantly in her building she had zero tolerance for racist behavior and wouldn't tolerate any of that garbage one bit—her brain didn't even work in that fashion. "People are people," she said. I was immediately reminded of my mother, who would say the same thing all the time, that people are people and that there are good people and bad people. That's it.

The elevator arrived. Its doors are brass, with an art

deco design carved into them. On the way up to the third floor she told me that she wants my room to be comfortable, and how she hated to rent rooms that are not taken care of because a lot of people here come from environments where "things are very depressed and a lot of people are losing their jobs and there's a lot of friction." They come here, she said, "and I say as long as you're staying here, this is your home, and please think of it as your home, I want to make it homelike and not just another hotel room. You know what I mean?" I nod yes while thinking about that. "I think this is the only way that people can survive here. I don't know what it's like out there in California, but these are bad times here."

The room she showed me was 315. The room had my name on it. Somebody had carved U FUCK UP deep in the red-painted door, and she opened it up and it was perfect— like warm freshly baked bread straight out of the oven, small bathroom with a sink, toilet, and shower, a closet, a bedroom with bed next to a chair and desk, an old-school radiator room heater by the window. The walls looked like they'd been painted white at least a hundred times, and had two framed twentieth-century Expressionist pieces of art nailed to them. Both pieces looked exactly like something you would find at the Salvation Army, Goodwill, or the Museum of Modern Art in New York. Four white walls and a window. That was it. Very postmodern. I loved it.

What's strange though, was that the apartment was laid out exactly like the one I lived at in San Francisco. It was also the same price as the studio apartment in Los

Angeles where I lived when I first moved out of my parents' house over a decade ago. Well, that apartment was actually a bit smaller than this space—a lot smaller—but it had a great view of the Hollywood sign, and I remember waking up in the mornings looking up at that thing and thinking, Well, at least I'm in Hollywood. How bad could it be, you know?

When I looked out the window here under overcast conditions, I saw that there was a breathtaking view across the freeway to the Cass Corridor. A couple street people were walking around as if they were lost on their way to the methadone clinic. I turned to her with a smile and said that it was perfect, above and beyond my expectations, and that I'd take it. She cheered up and told me that was great, and that whatever I did, not to go over there past the freeway. "We have kind of a raunchy ripe environment over there," she said soberly, and then offered to get me a television for my room, no problem, and I instinctively cut her off by telling her no—that wasn't necessary, I didn't like TV and could live perfectly fine, if not better, if I didn't have one.

Are you sure?

Yes, definitely.

I'm not one of those elitists who tells everyone they know how they don't have a television set so that they can think they're so much better than others for not having one. I just don't want one because there's really nothing on that I care to watch, so what's the point? It'd just take up space on my desk, and I need that for my laptop. And beer and wine bottles, ashtray, etc. Less is more.

Ever since I moved out of my parents' house over a decade ago, I've always sought out the cheapest available apartment to live in, even if it meant living in a neighborhood that most people would never consider moving into. I never once really thought anything of it, but my mother was the only one who ever figured it out and knew exactly why this all was.

"You always choose to live in tiny apartments in garbage neighborhoods because you think that's the best you can do. You never think big. It's okay to pay a little bit more, get bigger place, live better, work harder. But you think you're no good. That's why you choose to live like that. Those people have no choice. You're choosing to live that way."

On the way down the elevator, the Dutch lady views my ring and asked me if I was married, while smiling. I told her that I was. Happily, even.

"She doesn't mind you being here?"

"No. Well, she's a bit nervous about me being in Detroit. She doesn't want me to get shot here."

Mrs. Harrington assured me that I would be fine here at her hotel, and joking around she asked if I knew who was spreading the rumor of Detroit's rough reputation.

Not knowing the answer, I shrugged.

•

Once back down in the lobby, she also told me about her breakfast café, which she'd just opened up; two dollars for eggs and coffee was their special, along with a full breakfast menu. Her husband even had the idea that if you lived in the building and paid your rent on time, you'd get a free breakfast. I asked her how that was going, and she told me not so good; right now there were creative differences, if you will, going on with her and her cook, who lived in the building and was allowed to stay there rent-free as long as he worked at the café. She had a certain vision for the café, coffee and good breakfast food, but the cook wanted to cook soul food instead.

"I gave him all of the books and told him to make breakfast this way, do this, do that, and start making good smells, like bake your own apple pies, and he just sits there. Some people are good entrepreneurs and artists," she told me, "and some people have to work for someone else." She kindly added that he's a really nice guy, and makes really nice food, "when he can."

With all the people coming into and out of the building, I felt like I was at a cocktail party, being introduced to a bunch of people that I didn't know yet. All were kind, and she introduced me to every single one, all of whom she knew by name. We shook hands, and she told me what they do and a little bit about each. Like this five-foot-something arty Japanese hipster kid who hardly spoke any English at all and was always happy and smiling. He just ended up here while traveling. She then introduced me to a black guy "who's a well-known comedian. They tell me that he's fantastic," she said. "One of these days I'm going to get dressed up and go see him!"

I've stayed in a lot of hotels just like this, and this was the first time I came across one where the owner cared about the people who lived in her building. It was like they were all a part of her extended family: she knew them, and they knew her.

The comedian who lived in the building was actually playing at some legendary club in Detroit on New Year's Eve. It was a block away, and when he invited me to his show, I told him that I was not quite sure if I'd be able to make it, since I might be off to another city by then. Mrs. Harrington told me, "Well, who knows, you might fall in love with Detroit and decide not to leave."

We shared a chuckle, though in the back of my mind I must say I thought, anything can happen, I guess. I did join the military in a time of war never thinking that I ever would, and I did become a father without ever thinking that would happen either, so I guessed I couldn't really rule out any possibilities. Just then a white guy walked in the door, forties, very relaxed casual air and dress, and she brought me over to him and introduced me as a "writer from California." She then told me that he was an architect who used to live out in Hamtramck and moved into the building a couple months ago.

Mrs. Harrington then suggested that he show me around Detroit some time. He said he could do that, no problem, and then asked me what I was up to right now. I told him I wasn't up to anything, just hanging out, and he asked me if I wanted to go with him right now on a walk around the city, and he could take me to his work downtown. And just like that, we were off to discover Detroit.

•

Once outside the hotel, I asked my new acquaintance what kind of architecture he did. "Whatever comes down the tube," he said.

At the corner he pointed to a bar down the street, surrounded by empty lots, and told me that he did that bar. They gutted the building, and he did the interior. Prior to that the building was just a flophouse. A couple vagrants were just hanging out, not really doing anything, so I asked him about the neighborhood.

"A lot of crooks in this town."

"Like breaking-into-cars kind of stuff?"

"No, like gank you and take your money kind of stuff."

"Really?"

"Oh, yeah. I got a friend from Louisiana who came here, and he got mugged on his way to that bar. Took his wallet and watch."

He told me that all these vacant lots around us are now all "surface level" parking spaces for the sporting events. They all used to have buildings sitting on them, but they figured out that they could make more money converting them into parking spaces and charging twenty dollars to park there whenever a concert or sporting event happens, so they just tore them all down instead of boarding them up, like the handful of buildings that still remain on this street.

As we made our way down Park Avenue, no one in sight, he told me that all the bars were doing really slow business, now that baseball season was over. He added that back in the day the street we were on used to be a hangout for the

Purple Gang, Jewish mobsters who were rumrunners in the 1920s.

We passed by an empty storefront that carried a sign indicating a pizza restaurant coming soon, but a sign next to that indicated that all construction for that pizza restaurant had been halted, and as we walked through Grand Circus Park, which was like an outdoor break room for panhandlers, he told me that right now they were filming a movie downtown. I had noticed a lot of film trucks and production vehicles driving around. He said they were filming the new *Red Dawn* movie here, and he thought the story line for this one was something along the lines of the Chinese taking over America. "But if you think about it, they already have. Just go to Walmart, we don't make anything anymore."

When we stepped inside the lobby of his building, he told me that it had been an office building, but that right now eighty percent of the building was empty. While we waited for the elevator, I asked when this particular building was built, since I liked how the lobby was designed, and he told me that it was developed at the height of the art deco period. "The days of making buildings like this one are over," he said. "And they'll never come again."

"Why not?"

"You couldn't make this building now. All the marble, steel, plating, everything, you couldn't match it now. You'd go broke. Not anymore. Now everything is made cheap."

His office was located up on one of the top floors and had a spectacular panoramic view of all of Detroit; since the weather was clear, you could see for miles in all directions. He explained the layout of Detroit to me, saying that it's based on a wheel system. All the streets—Woodward, Gratiot, Michigan—start here in downtown but go out for miles and miles, all the way to the suburbs. He told me where all the neighborhoods were, which ones are which, Greektown, Hamtramck, Grosse Pointe, Midtown, East Detroit, Dearborn, and even Canada.

He then pointed to a building with a blue awning across the street and told me that it used to be a homeless shelter until it closed down not long ago. They gave out free food to all the bums, and all these bums would come down here from off Cass to get their free food, and of course the local businesses didn't care for that too much, since it was drawing the bums in. Now that the shelter was not there anymore, fewer homeless people came around. So that meant nobody came around.

He pointed out the many buildings around us that were bankrupt, one right after another. "That one's bankrupt, that one's bankrupt, that one's bankrupt, too, that one over there is pretty close, that one over there is, that one I'm pretty sure is, I think, that one is, that one, too. . . . What we're trying to do is get a population in here instead of just emptiness."

When I asked what they had in mind, he pointed out a building. "You mean the one that looks like a middle finger?" I asked. He told me that I was correct.

"We're doing that building. It's the old *Free Press* building."

"What are you guys going to do with it?"

"Condos."

I tried not to cringe. It seemed like every single one of these buildings across our country that used to house things called jobs were now vacant, showing FOR SALE or LEASE signs, and were now being converted into condos or lofts. Perhaps they moved online, or to a different building? Who knows?

His boss, who was well dressed and looked like an architect, then pointed out the drafting plans for the *Free Press* building, which were sitting on a nearby table. I asked if I could take a look at them. He told me sure. The boss, who was wearing a scarf indoors, migrated over to me and in a calm voice explained, "Underground is going to be parking, the first floor is going to be retail, the second floor is going to be offices, and the rest are going to be apartments."

I then realized what he was showing me. It wasn't the floor plan to that building, it was the floor plan for this country—the beige condominium nightmare. That building used to have jobs inside it. Since those were all gone now or had moved somewhere else, the building was now empty. Since we don't know what to do with this building and all the others like it, they are all being converted into condos. I'm starting to think that we are all headed toward living in a country of beige condos and working service industry jobs, since those will be the only jobs left. One day I'm going to be tipping you, and you're going to be tipping me.

•

Back at the Park Avenue Hotel. Mrs. Harrington greeted me with a sweet smile, and introduced me to her husband of fifty years, an older white gentleman in his early eighties who was born and raised here in Detroit. With his enthusiastic knowledge of Detroit, Mr. Harrington reminded me a bit of my own grandfather, who was a great storyteller and historian of Maine, where he was born and raised. He knew everything Maine inside and out and loved it so much that he wanted his ashes spread there when he died.

In the lobby Mr. Harrington told me a bit about the history of the hotel. Ground was broken for the building in 1927, and it was finished in 1928. The architect was a guy named Louis Kamper, who also designed several other historic buildings here in town, such as the Book Tower and Book Cadillac. The people who built this building, as well as a couple others here in Detroit, all went bankrupt in the crash of 1929.

We stepped out on the sidewalk, and Mr. Harrington pointed out the Detroit Life Building, diagonally across the street. Detroit Life was all boarded up, vacant, and had a FOR LEASE sign on it. The Detroit Women's City Club right next to it was also vacant, boarded up, and had a FOR LEASE sign on it. "At one time that was the elite club for the women, you follow me?" he said, and explained to me that all these parking lots around his hotel once had bustling buildings sitting on them, but they had all been torn down.

He stopped himself for a moment, thought, and then

told me that it was good that they'd saved the automobile industry, because "a lot of other countries would love to have it." He added, "Where else can the not smartest guy in the world get a job and have almost a middle-class living?"

After that I walked back to the front desk and paid my rent to the guy working the desk, who also works for a nearby bail bondsman as a bill collector. I asked him a little bit more about the area, and he told me that as long as I didn't cross the freeway after dark and stayed mostly downtown, I'd be fine. Mrs. Harrington was also there in the lobby, and she told me that even during the day I shouldn't head over across the freeway. Right here in downtown, she explained, "We're like the Baghdad Green Zone," and if I looked at and thought of it that way, I'd be fine. But if I took my shit anywhere else, I'd be taking my chances. Across the freeway was what we called in the military "outside the wire."

Being no fan of the Green Zone, I thanked them both, stepped outside the hotel, and walked across the freeway.

It'd been a while since I'd stepped foot outside the wire, and the one thing I noticed was that there weren't a whole heck of a lot of grocery stores in the downtown area of Detroit. In fact, I hadn't found any other than a couple liquor stores that sold corn chips, canned food items, Obama gear, and that was it. I had no idea how in the world the people here got their food, and I remembered seeing a location over by Martin Luther King Boulevard with the word GROCERY painted on the exterior, near remnants of a burned-out building. So I decided to head that way.

A couple vacant lots nearby, homeless people were hanging out on benches and chairs. A nice handful of people were just hanging out in front of the building, and as I made my way toward it, I wondered if these were just ordinary people doing extraordinary things. I had my camera slung over my shoulder, and I thought about removing it and placing it in my backpack, but chose not to so as not to offend anyone. These guys were totally staring at me, and if I did put my camera away it would look like I did so because I thought they were criminals or up to no good just because they were black. Hanging out in front of a corner store on MLK Boulevard mid-workday didn't mean they were going to gank me. That's racist and feeds into a stereotype, I thought to myself. But as I walked toward the entrance, I still noticed that all their eyes were fixed on me, and it was a bit late to turn around or go the other way. As I got closer to them, they started taking a couple steps toward me. They didn't look happy, and when I got really close, one of them finally said, "What you need?"

What did I need? Good question. I needed groceries. Actually, no, what *you guys* here in Detroit need is a fucking grocery store, a Trader Joe's or something like that. For some weird reason I didn't tell them that, nor did I ask them for recommendations or directions to a decent supermarket that they might know of in the area. It didn't seem like that kind of relationship. And honestly, this whole scene had the makings of an ABC after-school special in it, and so instead I just kind of froze there for a split second, looked at them all, and then I did it. I said, "You guys seen a badge?"

"What?"

"I'm looking for my badge. I was here earlier, and I think I lost it here. Have you guys seen anything like that lying around here?"

"Muthafucka, *what*?!"

His sidekick then exclaimed to his friend, who was standing there on the corner, "Nigga here say he lost his *badge*?!"

Guy on the corner replied back, "Lost his badge?! Nigga, *what*?!"

Others looked over.

I again told them all, "Yeah, I'm looking for it. Excuse me." And I made my way between them and inside "Grocery."

Back home I live in the Tenderloin District, which in ways is kind of similar to this neighborhood. A friend of mine says that whenever he finds himself in situations like the one I was now in, he tells a joke, and they laugh, and everything is okay. And the joke he uses all the time is the I-lost-my-badge routine, but I think I completely fucked it up. I delivered my lines the way Clint Eastwood might have, when I was supposed to say them like maybe Will Ferrell or Dave Chapelle. Instead of laughing, these guys thought I was an obviously unarmed cop on foot with no backup.

Still in character, with my head down, walking around the aisles looking for my badge, I noticed that the only items that they sold were canned goods, a lot of which had a thick layer of dust on top of them, since they'd probably been on the shelves since Detroit was prosperous. No one was shopping for food here. People were dumping cans into these huge dishwasher-looking machines to get money for them, but the only thing sold inside this "grocery" was alcohol. Arabs worked the store, of course operating behind bulletproof glass, and when I looked back outside, the guys were pointing to me and telling another buddy that I was looking for my badge. When I stepped outside, I kind of scanned the parking lot and area around me, noticed that they were all just staring at me, heads cocked, with these really confused expressions on their faces, and I proceeded to walk away as quickly as possible without appearing to be walking away as quickly as possible.

Not too far away, while I was walking across a couple empty lots that used to be buildings, I noticed a black guy with several empty beer bottles in his hands. He looked like he was in a good mood, and the two of us were headed in the same direction, so when he started to veer his way over to the corner liquor store I asked him if they took cans. He told me that they did. I thanked him, and a couple steps later, walking across another vacant lot with my head down again, I came across dozens of empty bottles of hard liquor just sitting there. They were all over the place. Free money. As I was gathering them up in my arms so I could do what he just did, he showed up again, and I asked him if they'd take these as well. He told me no, they just take empty beer bottles. Bummed that there was no financial incentive for me to recycle, I let all the empty liquor bottles clang back to the ground. He then asked me where I was from. I told him California, and he extended his hand for a handshake that ended with a soulful hand snap.

"Welcome to Detroit," he said.

CHAPTER THIRTEEN

Mission from God

"The cure for boredom is curiosity. There is no cure for curiosity."

DOROTHY PARKER

"What is the difference between exploring and being lost?"

DAN ELDON

I brought a camera with me on this little road trip of mine, and I'd hardly pulled the trigger to it till now. Here in Detroit I was dropping memory cards like dropping 5.62 M4 mags during a Mosul firefight. I was shooting all in black and white. When I think of the word *beat*, I think weathered and run-down to the point where it's beautifully depressing. And black and white just seems to fit perfectly here in this environment.

After a long day of amateur wannabe photojournalism, I called it quits. When I walked in to the lobby, the doorman buzzed me in through the heavy steel gate, and from there I took the elevator up to the third floor. I had some cheap wine with me, since earlier in the day I had come across a going-out-of-business sale downtown and picked up a couple bottles of red. I unlocked the door and walked in. The door self-locks when you close it, and after turning on the lights I released my keys from my hand, dropping them clanging to the floor. Instinctively I did this behavior as well back in my old studio apartment in San Francisco so I don't lose my keys or spend thirty minutes looking around for them whenever I want to leave. I just bend down and pick them up.

I had purchased a roll of toilet paper earlier in the day, which I placed in the bathroom, and after that I set my backpack on my desk, opened it up, put my laptop on it, turned it on, and, while waiting for it to start, grabbed a corkscrew from my backpack and opened up a bottle. Since I have no cups or silverware I drank straight out of the bottle, which is fine. I then walked over to the window, cracked it, and lit up a smoke.

While drinking, I downloaded all the photographs that I had taken onto my desktop. I looked at my watch. I had a couple minutes left till last call. Since both bottles of wine were now expired, I picked up my keys off the floor and went back downstairs to the bar on the first floor.

I then spent the night sleeping on the blue two-seater sofa in my room, because I had gotten so wasted that I couldn't find my bed. I took a shower—although the hot water was lukewarm at best—then I put some least-dirty clothes on and decided to go downstairs so that I could "Buy Local" and support Mrs. Harrington's café by ordering breakfast. I'm socially conscious that way.

The cook was a young black guy in his twenties, and he seemed friendly. Ordered an omelet and coffee, tipped a couple bucks in the jar, and then went back to my room to grab my journal and camera.

During the day, there was always a lot of action going on in the lobby, people coming and going, and nine times out of ten Mrs. Harrington would be down there working on something. Today when I was on my way out some new furniture was being brought into the building, all wrapped in plastic, and a couple of people who lived in the building were helping to bring it inside. Mrs. Harrington asked me what I was up to today, and I told her that I was just going to go out and explore for a bit. She asked about my room and my stay in her hotel, and I told her that everything was great, perfect even.

For me it was, and if it wasn't perfect, I don't think that I could ever tell her it wasn't.

In the lobby I thought that'd be it, how's your room, oh it's great, that's good, let me know if you need anything, will do, thanks, kind of small talk, and that'd be it and I'd be off and on my way. Instead, Mrs. Harrington had a story to tell me.

The story that she had for me today was an incident that had just recently happened; a couple days before, in fact. What happened was there was such a bad smell coming from one of the rooms that the other tenants on the floor were actually complaining about it. So she went up, found out what room it was coming from, and saw that the person had a bunch of decaying food in her fridge, which wasn't even plugged in. So Mrs. Harrington tossed all the old food out and removed the fridge, brought it outside so she could wash it thoroughly. Well, the tenant came home, saw that her fridge was gone, and called the cops. When the cops showed up, they told Mrs. Harrington that they could throw her in jail for what she'd just done, that you legally couldn't just go inside somebody's room like that. Well, she couldn't believe it. Something smelled like death, and the other tenants were up in arms about it—she couldn't just do nothing about it! And so with great pride she told me what she told the cops, which was, "Fine, go ahead and throw me in jail." Which they didn't, of course. But she told her husband that if there was a next time, she'd happily go to jail, and she even told him not to bail her out, that she'd do the time.

I smiled and wished her well, she did the same back to me, and I exited the hotel, imagining at the same time my Korean mother operating a motel such as the Park Ave. I could see her running it in the same fashion, which made me chuckle to myself.

•

On the other side of the freeway was a neighborhood called Brush Park, and you could tell that it was a historic district just by looking at the houses, which were now all boarded up, vacant, and half dead. Victorian, Georgian, Italianate, French Renaissance, Gothic Revival—all built in the late 1800s, all situated on spacious lots with front and back yards, and each had a "Building Detroit's Past into the Future" sign posted in front of it, with an image of what the house would look like if restored. A homeless guy slept in an entryway. Most of these mansions appeared left for dead, as if an artillery shell had gone off in the living room. I wondered why that was. Only one or two of them were fixed up and had people living in them. The rest sat there like old tombstones in a battered cemetery.

After taking photos of a castle, I continued walking

along the street and came across a front porch where an old black couple were hanging out. The black guy was a bit older, wore a sun-faded old Detroit Lions hat, and the lady had bright red lipstick and a phone book sitting open on her lap. She was calling up places, trying to locate a part or something for her Ford. I said hello to them, and since the two of them had seen me taking snapshots of the castle, the guy told me that it used to belong to the infamous Detroit Piston Dennis Rodman.

"Really?" I said. "He used to own that?"

"Sure did," he said. "And he would buy some shit like that, too."

I looked back over at it; it was virtually destroyed.

"If he bought that, why in the hell didn't he fix it up then?"

"Ha!"

The man had a nice infectious laugh, which made me laugh. I looked around, and you could tell that at one time this neighborhood had been the Beverly Hills of this city.

"How did this neighborhood turn to shit?" I asked. "How come people aren't moving in and fixing these houses up?"

The lady on the phone, interrupting her call by telling the other person to please hold on, told me, "Because they wanted to turn this neighborhood into a parking lot for the two stadiums and destroy a historic district without being accountable."

All nonchalant, she unflustered herself and went back to talking to whomever she was talking to.

"Where you from?" the guy asked me. "And how long

you been here?" With his head cocked and one eyebrow raised, he then asked what I'd heard about Detroit, and more specifically from whom. Everything I said was the funniest thing the guy had ever heard.

"I heard on the other side of that street is called the Cass Corridor."

"And what they say about that?"

"Don't go there."

Hysterical laughter.

"Yeah, I'm serious, everyone's told me that whatever I do, don't go over there."

Laughing so hard he can hardly speak. "Who say that?" Laughing. *"Who told you that?"*

"Umm, you know. . . ."

I knew where he was going with this, especially when he stopped laughing and gave me a serious look. "What kind of people you talking to?" he asked.

"You know"—I had a difficult time answering—"people. . . ."

Then I pointed over toward downtown with my finger.

With his head cocked again, he asked, "Mainstream white people?"

"Yup," I told him. "Mainstream white people."

More hysterical laughter.

Well, a couple of black people had told me the same thing, but I completely forgot about that since I was laughing along with him. After he was done laughing, he told me all about how the Cass Corridor back in the day was an area mostly frequented by white people, and that it was somewhat of a red light district back then. That's originally how it got its bad reputation, "from white people." Since it was also some-what of a bohemian neighborhood, blacks didn't really hang out there too much because they weren't welcomed there. When the riots happened in '67, "the whites exodused the city—their conscience bothered them about treating black folks so wrong for decades and centuries, and after the riot they flew outta here like it was an epidemic. But they still have this social need to come back to the city almost on a daily basis to the football games, to the baseball games, so it's somewhat of a psyche thing with most whites when it comes to the city, especially the inner city."

Wondering if white folks were moving back down here, he told me that the city was trying to entice them. "It's a rebirth now, on the rebound. They cleared out most of all the crack houses and projects," he said. "You see, they moved the blacks out of this area. They've done all sorts of wicked things to get the blacks out—they've busted pipes, DTE came in and cut black peoples' lights off, made them move, they tricked this one woman here, you see that big place over there?" I looked over; it was a beautiful Victo-rian house, now boarded up. "They tricked her out of her property; she's in a convalescent home now. They've been doing this for the last fifteen years here."

The lady then turned away again from her call to inform me, "They're all a bunch of crooks, thieves, and liars! They're pimping the federal government for federal funds, and that's what the whole game is about. That why Obama is giving money—the people don't get the money, only the wealthy and the 'fluent get the money, and it never trickles down. All it is a rape of the federal government of federal funds, and they use poor people as a red carpet to get it. They pimp 'em, they say you sit here and you gotta stay here and you gotta be poor so I can keep asking the government for more money. It's a vicious cycle."

She went back again to talking to whoever she was talking to on the phone, and the guy schooled me by saying, "Now you got to remember that urban renewal means *blacks removed*. It means move all the blacks out and bring in upscale middle-class mainstream white folks. By whatever means necessary."

Taking note, I thanked the couple for chatting with me, and while I was going on my way the lady hung up her phone and called after me, and what she told me would be the pearl that Detroit graciously handed to me. "Now, let me tell you something—never believe what people tell you, young man. Always seek out knowledge and truth for your own self and never believe what they say about a person. You learn about that person for yourself, and never, ever be afraid to go somewhere. That's a bunch of bull crap. When somebody tells you don't go—you *go*. How you going to know if you don't go?"

CHAPTER FOURTEEN

Unsuccessful Men with Talent

*"Live as if you were to die tomorrow. Learn as if
you were to live forever."*

MOHANDAS GANDHI

Walking and talking on my iPhone, the daily check-in
phone call to my wife, assuring her that I'm still alive and/
or not in jail, while passing by gray burned-down houses
and houses that appear to be boarded up and empty, I
could hear our son crying in the background. I was report-
ing to her that everything was cool and that I was doing
well, people here were great, when I spotted a huge cement
structure a couple blocks away over by the train tracks. It
was concrete block, ten or so stories high and wide, just sitting there, of course, liké so much else in this city, abandoned. Once I got closer, I saw "Division of Beatrice Foods
Co." on the side of it. I told my wife that I had to get off the
phone because I wanted to go inside and explore. She told
me to be careful.

·

I climbed up into the building through a loading dock.
Inside, it was dark and cold. I looked around to see if
there was anybody else here. It was silent, and I didn't see

anybody. I stood there listening; all I heard was emptiness. So I started walking. The deeper I got into the building, the darker it got, to beyond pitch-black levels. I had no idea what in the world I was stepping on half the time, could have been a dead body for all I knew, but every so often pinpricks of light would penetrate from the sides. I could hear each crackling step echo and bounce off all the cement walls, and the temperature was a lot cooler in here as well; I found it all to be very peaceful, calming even. Of course, it looked like a couple Scud missiles had gone off in here. Enormous chunks of gray concrete were scattered throughout, parts of the cement roof that had caved in. As I was taking snapshots of the freight elevator amid this decomposing carcass of a structure, I suddenly froze. My pupils immediately dilated as my heart rate skyrocketed. I was not alone.

I listened. My ears heard footsteps; I slowly turned to look. I didn't see anybody or anything, so I listened again. The sound was coming from around a cement pillar and wall.

I should have been scared, but I wasn't. I was curious, and in my curiosity, which hopefully wouldn't lead to my death, I found myself walking slowly, as slowly as possible, one soft step at a time, toward the sound. I walked with my heels gently touching the ground first, slowly rolling the rest of my shoe's sole forward, cringing at every sound that a pebble or shard of shattered glass made while I stepped over it. It took me nearly ten minutes to walk forty meters, since noise discipline was my utmost concern right now, so as to not give up my position. When I reached the corner the sound was coming around from, I stood there for a second, then slowly turned the corner.

A black guy wearing a beanie stood in front of me with what seemed to be several greasy jackets. Next to him was a hole in the cement that measured about fifteen by fifteen feet and went into the ground at least twenty feet, filled at the bottom with filthy water, and he appeared to be getting ready to go to work, though I didn't know exactly what that was yet.

He was rolling up his sleeves, and was not one bit alarmed when he saw me. I saw him, he saw me, and we both said hello to each other, the same way two strangers would if they ran into each other at a bus stop. He looked me over for a second, then asked if I had any smokes. I handed him one which he thanked me for and after giving him a light, to spark up conversation I asked about Detroit. "Bad, really bad here," he told me.

As he was obviously a man of few words, I tried to pry more out of him by asking, "How did you end up here?"

"It happened, man." He shrugged while exhaling. "Really, it was all my fault. You know?"

The hole he was standing in front of was near pitch-black. If you strained your eyes, you could make out that it was full of murky water, and that there was scrap metal and jagged debris down there. I hate to be using *Star Wars* references, but it looked exactly like the *Star Wars* garbage compactor down there, the scene where the walls start coming together. I stood there silently watching as the guy made his way down into the hole, using an old wooden ladder. Where he was going, to me, looked like an ideal location to stash a dead body, and I had a bad feeling about what I was about to witness. I asked if it would be okay to just hang out and watch him do whatever he was about to do, and he said sure.

In horror I watched as the guy lowered his body all the way into the hole, more than 80 percent of his body submerged in the filthy water at the heart of this massive abandoned concrete building. He started running his hands underneath the water, looking for something. "Pipes," he said, which you could hear rattle and echo throughout the building whenever he found one. One by one, he began to pull them dripping out of the murk and set them over to the side.

These copper pipes were about ten or so feet long, and looked heavy. As I was taking pictures and hoping that this guy has gotten his TB shots, a buddy of his rolled up with an industrial belt to help gather up all the pipes. Black guy, old and weathered, just like his old sun-faded Detroit Lions hat, and he was wearing thrashed clothing from head to toe. He also was unfazed when he met me and also greeted me with a kind hello. "Got any smokes?" he asked. I handed him one, and since now I have to know, I asked, "What are you guys doing?"

"We're pulling pipes out." Copper piping is pretty valuable, which answered my question of why they are doing this. He explained, "What they do is, they put acid on them, kill all the bacteria. They got to redo them because if they don't they can't sell, because they be toxic."

Okay, if those pipes were extremely toxic, and this guy was submerged in that water to get to them, then he was pretty much fucked and probably wouldn't be bouncing grandkids on his knee.

We stood and watched the man in the pool of water. My eyes adjusted to the surreal scene. His friend didn't seem inclined to join him down there. His demeanor was very calm, and he smoked his cigarette the very same way that he talked, which was long, deep drags and slowly. And slowly he explained why they had to do this. "They took all the jobs away. People got to do day labor and sometimes you can't do day labor so you just have to make your jobs—make pallets, you know, you get two dollars a pallet and you have to make everything just about the way they was if they brought them off the factory, you know? Say you go buy a house that cost fifty, forty thousand dollars, how in the hell can you pay over six or four hundred dollars a month? So you gotta get out here, out in the streets, and sell metal, you gotta pick up bottles, you got to go build pallets. It's all kinds of stuff, man. Some guys can hardly eat, man, really. They get them little foods at them food banks and it's not enough to last more than one day and the guy's starving again if he got two or three kids. *Shit.* He got to buy shoes, clothes for them and try and send 'em to school. That's why these little kids are so bad, man. They half starving. It's worse here than in any foreign country."

"What'd you do before?"

Slowly exhaling, he sadly told me, "I worked at GM, man.

"I've been here all my life, and I don't know. I'm thinking about going to Toronto. I like it up there. It ain't bad up there like it is down here, man. People still working, you can work in a cannery or on a tuna boat, stuff like that. I work at the market part time on Saturday and that still ain't enough to pay for nothin' 'cause utilities are so high that's what eats everybody's money up. Gas, electric, and all those expenses, man, you work all day and you ain't got nothin'."

•

Since I was now out of smokes, I asked them if they knew of a corner store. They gave me directions to one a couple blocks away, and when I asked them if they needed anything like a pop, they both said yeah, but then quickly changed their order over to beer. The guy pulling the pipes out wanted a Bud, the guy hanging out chatting with me wanted Milwaukee's Best. After I took their orders and told them I'd be right back, they told me not to go quite yet, and that they'd give me a ride. They were expecting a ride to show up any second now, and sure enough, after a couple minutes, one did. A beat-to-hell bombed-out Ford Taurus that looked straight out of the junkyard was driven by this really skinny, tough-looking black lady with these really intense eyes and crazy hair. She pulled up and honked her horn. The guy who was pulling the pipes out of the hole, drenched, threw on his coats and ran over to the car while telling me to hurry and jump in. So I did, the other black guy came as well, and we arranged ourselves in the back seat, which was completely thrashed. The lady who was driving turned around in her seat and just glared at me. I said hello, nervously waved even, and she didn't respond. She then looked over at the guy who'd been pulling the pipes out and was now sitting in the front passenger seat, still completely drenched and dripping into the upholstery, and shot this look at him, this look that clearly said, *Who*

*the fuck is this off-duty police-officer-lookin' muthafucka
who is now all up in the back seat of my muthafuckin' car?!*

He told her to relax and soulfully said, "He's with me.
It's *coo*. We go to the stow real quick." She didn't respond
till he exclaimed, "Come on, let's go!" She then angrily put
it in drive, still looking not one bit happy about all this, and
just like that I was off with my new friends. People here in
Detroit are nice.

On our way to wherever they were going to take me, I
heard the doors lock, and my friend sitting next to me in
the back seat leaned over and told me that where we were
going, "Don't be taking no pictures if I was you." I thanked
him for the advice. Told him not to worry about that. That
I was a professional, and I knew exactly what I was doing.

We passed by a truck-stop-looking white lady wearing old faded blue jeans and a thrashed flannel shirt, kind
of tweaking out, just standing in the street in front of an
abandoned house, scanning every car that drove by with
the same look in her eyes that most hookers who are strung
out on whatever illegal substance have in their eyes when
they're working. On the other side of the street from where
we parked was a row of chairs all along the sidewalk, with
people sitting in them, just hanging out, drinking alcohol
out of brown paper bags. At least a dozen of them. It was
midday. I wondered about open container laws here in Detroit, and I had to think hard: What day of the week was
this? Except for the laborers I was with, nothing in this
neighborhood would tell you whether it was a day of work
or a day of rest. I liked that. On the opposite street corner, a
couple young black youths were hanging out. They looked

tough, and there was a girl standing there on the opposite street corner, kind of hefty, tight jeans, heels, and wearing a tight pink tube top, which wasn't doing her any favors. As much as I wanted to take photographs of all this, since it was all sooo beautifully authentic, I chose not to. Which sadly made me realize that I don't have what it takes to one day become a photojournalist for *National Geographic*. Instead I tucked my camera inside my coat and zipped it up. The guy seated in the back seat next to me leaned back over to me and said, "That's a good idea."

We parked over by a liquor store. The record then kind of skipped as I got out of the car, and the people sitting down all in a row in their chairs alongside the road seemed to stop what they were doing and just stare at me. A part of me wondered if they really were staring at me, or if that was just my self-consciousness, thinking that they were staring at me. So I stared at them to find out. They all looked pissed. Yup, they were staring at me.

·

My friends and I all walked into the corner store together. On a wall inside was a mural devoted to Obama, and of course the Middle Eastern guys working the counter were behind bulletproof glass, and the two guys I was with changed their minds on the beer and asked instead if they could have sandwiches, since they were hungry. I told them that was no problem at all, and after I picked up my pack of smokes and paid for everything, we drove back.

The lady backed the car up alongside the building, collapsed the back seat down, and opened up the trunk, and the three of them started shoving the copper pipes into the back of the car with their bare hands.

As I took pictures, the black lady grabbed a pipe and asked me if I was from Detroit.

"No, I'm from California."

"Oh," she said. "You probably don't see this out in California, now do you?"

I think about that for a second and then tell her that we recycle, too.

She laughed, but it wasn't really a laugh-at-a-funny-joke kind of laugh, but one of those tough-as-nails laughs, a those-people-ain't-shit-out-in-California kind of laugh.

"If Californians came here, they wouldn't know how to survive, now would they, huh?" she said.

I told her that she was probably correct on that one. Probably all starve to death, since there's no Whole Foods within Rollerblading or Razor scooter distance.

With the copper pipes filling the back of the car, she drove off, and the guy pulling the pipes out, who went by the name Popcorn, went back into the hole to pull more pipes out, and the guy wearing the old Detroit Lions hat and I sat around, smoked, and talked a bit more.

I asked him how much they made doing this, and he told me that he got paid by the weight. He estimated that today they might make sixty dollars. He told me they could make a whole heck of a lot more if they had the right tools, or any tools for that matter. He then looked up at the ceiling. There were all sorts of piping and tubing and metal up there. "You see, that's good money right there.

You see that up there, all the way to the end, you looking at five or six tons, but you need the right kinds of tools to cut it." He told me they could make a fortune if they just had the right tools.

"The guy that owns this building, he don't mind for us to take stuff outta here," he said, "because he want it out to make way for the demolition crew. He's a good guy."

He had a cloth sack slung over his shoulder, and after I'd said good-bye and thanks for letting me hang with them, he took off walking.

As I was leaving, I took some exterior shots of the massive building. A black guy just walking along the road by himself saw me, and I thought he was going to ask me for a smoke, or if I had any change, but I was wrong.

"Great building, ain't it?" he said as he passed.

"Yeah, it really is."

•

On my walk back, I came across Detroit's meatpacking district, which converts on the weekends into a farmer's market, and after passing an Islamic slaughterhouse, I spotted an Ethiopian buffet. Ever since realizing you could eat Ethiopian food with your hands I've been a fan, and since I was a bit hungry, I walked inside. The lone girl working, who seemed about my age, told me that it was ten dollars, eat all you want, so I did. I sat down at a table in the back corner, and my camera was sitting there on the table. As I was eating, the girl came over and asked me if I'm a photographer.

I didn't know how to answer that one. With digital cameras, everybody is a goddamn photographer now, so I told her no, I wasn't a photographer, I was just an enthusiast who liked going inside all these abandoned buildings here in Detroit and taking photos of the beauty I found, and that gave me a reason to explore inside them. She sat down at my table, introducing herself, and told me that she enjoyed doing the very same thing. She told me of a couple other spots nearby that were good to explore, as well as an abandoned school over by where she lived, and that when they shut it down they left everything inside it—all the desks, books, everything—and she couldn't understand why they did that. They could have sold or donated everything inside the school, but instead they just left it all there for people to take. She herself had grabbed a couple desks. The books, which were all expensive and could have been put back into circulation or donated to the library or to another school, were just left there to rot. "Sad," she said. When I left, she invited me to a Harvest Festival in her neighborhood later that month. I thanked her and made my way back to the hotel.

•

At the hotel, Mrs. Harrington was hanging out in the lobby, talking with the guy working the front desk. I was greeted by her warm smile. She curiously asked me what I'd discovered today here in Detroit. I told her all about the guys I met inside the abandoned building, and showed her a couple of the photographs that I took inside. She put her reading glasses on, looked at them, and her smile disappeared into a look of grave concern for my personal safety.

In a motherly way, she gasped while putting her hand over her heart and warned me sternly several times to be extremely careful doing this, it was not safe for me to be exploring in and around these places, especially all by myself.

I ignored her the same way that I ignored my mother every time she put in a request for me to quit smoking. "It's fine, Mrs. Harrington," I said. "Nothing's going to happen to me." That wasn't the answer she wanted to hear, and that look of concern was still cemented on her face as I made my way to the elevator and took it up to my room.

·

The Park Ave. had wireless, which was great. A lot of these weekly or monthly hotels don't, you have to go to a coffee shop or some fancy hotel lobby and pick up their signal to get online. Using the satellite images on Google Maps, I took a top view of the city and found myself searching for parts of Detroit that looked industrial and depressing. Like how North Korea looks on Google Maps. Sadly, there were a lot of those areas in Detroit. Using pen and paper, I marked down locations to explore, since my heart was now dead set on exploration of our greatest industrial relics. This would have been my dream when I was a kid, to do something like this someday. There, in the room with U FUCK UP scratched deeply on my door, inside one of the greatest hotels in the country, I felt lucky.

With a fully charged battery and two empty memory cards, my camera and I set off for the Packard auto plant. The night before, I'd read up on the place for a bit. It had first opened in 1903, closing its doors in 1957. At one time it was considered the "most modern automobile manufacturing facility in the world." It was located on East Grand Avenue, on thirty-five acres of land, and occupied 3,500,000 square feet.

You could put a lot of condos in that space.

When I arrived, I parked the Caliente by an archway over the street, which at one time read "Motor City Industrial Park." Each letter had been painted on a pane of glass, and since some of those windows were now shattered, it read like that one game show where you select a letter and guess the word or phrase.

I was amazed by how far it stretched, a city unto itself. This place opened just at the start of the human experiment with the automobile, and it must have seemed like a permanent monument to American primacy. A century later, the whistling wind was its only sound, and it sat next to a cemetery in the middle of a quiet residential community.

After I parked my car on a side road, I got out and walked toward an open door. I looked around: residential houses, lawns, birds chirping, a family car or two parked on the street. When I took my first step inside, it felt as if I was stepping into a whole other planet. It was like walking into a building the Allies had bombed during World War II. Some spaces were littered with trash, some were not, and some were like theme rooms. One room was nothing but old smashed-to-hell television sets from the 1970s, and another room was nothing but old tires. A couple rooms had absolutely nothing inside them, and then all of a sudden you'd come across a room with several old boats just sitting on the workroom floor, spray-painted. Bags of trash here and there. In one room, somebody had spray-painted in careful cursive, "What happened here?" The hallways and rooms were endless; they seemed to go on and on forever.

At one time, we actually made things within these walls; people made a good living and worked in teams and shipped items off our assembly lines. Now the Packard plant and the ruins of Detroit are large open coffins where artists and vagrants pay their respects, or gravediggers come in to pick a corpse of its copper bones, or people dump yesterday's garbage, or amateur photographers practice f-stops and shutter speeds and find perfect locations for Urban Exploration.

•

Kerouac had his great enthusiasms, but none greater than jazz, and the improvised life, and the lovely notion of being alive—*alive*—moment to moment. Now jazz is something of a museum piece, not as alive as it once was. But these things that have been left for dead from a different America—they are *alive*, and merit exploration. At least for me they do.

The America that Kerouac escaped into was vast, anonymous, and disconnected from one part to the next. It was a place that matched his reckless, restless energy. His rootlessness was a celebration of freedom, a throwing-off of the shackles of convention, the only limits being how much your liver could stand. In the America of his discovery, there were no more bad wars, our wealth was measured in tangible gold bars, and gleaming massive cars like my Caliente were rolling off an endless assembly line that stretched from here to heaven. This prosperity would never, ever end. Or so they thought.

•

Walking from one room to the next room, I came across a quote printed on a piece of old card stock. "Press On," read the card. Underneath that, it read, "Nothing in the world can take the place of persistence. Talent will not; nothing is more common than unsuccessful men with talent. Genius will not; unrewarded genius is almost a proverb. Education will not; the world is full of educated derelicts. Persistence and Determination alone are omnipotent."

The card was just lying there on the ground, all by itself in the middle of this huge vacant cement-walled room inside an even larger abandoned factory that used to employ thousands of Americans. I wondered how long it had been sitting there, since there was a thick film of dust on it. After taking a photograph of the card in its natural setting, I folded it up and put it in my back pocket. As I was exploring the building, taking pictures, listening to the camera shutter echo against all the cement walls and long dust-covered hallways that went on for days every time I clicked a snapshot, I wondered how that quote ended up here, lost in Detroit.

I'm assuming you probably don't see too many "the world is full of educated derelicts" quotes posted up on the commons walls of the Ivy League, where people tend to pride themselves on being overeducated—but where I can see a quote like that being posted is on an old dirty fridge at a small auto shop, or in the break room at the assembly line, places where people could once make an honest living without a college education. It takes persistence to wake up every morning and work a hard, thankless job day in and out.

•

With one memory card full, the juice nearly drained from my camera, and only about a third, if that, of the Packard plant explored, I decided to go back to the hotel to safely download everything onto my hard drive, come back the following day, and keep on coming back till every single room here was fully explored.

On my way in, I ran into Mrs. Harrington, and she told me that it had been busy today; the phone had been ringing off the hook with people calling to ask about vacancies. The city just recently shut down three of their homeless shelters, and a lot of new people needed a place to stay. She told me that she wouldn't rent a room to someone that didn't have a job, that she's tried in the past to rent out to people without employment and it was very problematic and just one big hassle, so she no longer does that.

"How was your day, Colby?" she then asked.

I told her about the Packard auto plant, and showed her a couple pictures from my camera.

In shock, "You went again all by yourself?"

"Yeah."

She then of course told me again to be careful, it's highly unsafe, and you never know what could happen inside those buildings.

"I know."

When I got to my room, I stared at the "Press On" quote for a while, then set it on my desk.

●

Like owning real estate, there's something very American about purchasing and owning an automobile. You have to pay money to have one, you have to pay money to keep it maintained, you have to pay money whenever it breaks down, you have to pay money for the insurance, you have to pay money every time you put fuel in the tank, whenever you receive a ticket, pass a toll booth, wash it, or park the fucking thing.

It all gives me a headache, the fact that everything costs money. It had been several years since I'd owned an auto-mobile, and now that I'd been reminded of all this once again, by the time I arrived in Detroit my enthusiasm for owning a car had all but disappeared. I lost that one somewhere around the Wyoming border. Sick and tired of paying for everything, I decided not to drive unless I had to and to leave the Caliente parked up on the top floor of the parking garage a block away from the hotel. Out of sight, out of mind.

While passing through Atlantic City, Iowa, I had pur-chased an old-school bicycle off an old-timer who owned and operated a corner bike shop. It was one of those beach cruiser kind of bikes with only one gear, and I really didn't need a bike, but since he was so nice and was only charging twenty bucks for it I picked it up. It's been stashed in my trunk ever since. So today I grabbed a wrench, put it back together, and went off on a bike ride.

Since I had been unable to explore the entire Packard

auto plant in one afternoon, I decided to ride my bike back over. While pedaling, I was passing one abandoned and burned-down building right after another.

I passed by the huge cement building I'd explored several days ago, when I saw one of the guys who'd been taking out pipes, the one with the decade-old Lions hat. We did the fist-bump greeting, and he asked me what I was up to. I told him that I was just riding my bike and on my way to check out another abandoned building. I asked what he was up to, and he told me that he was still pulling copper pipes out of that building. He asked how the writing's coming along, and I told him that it was going fine, and I'd come back and chill with him in a couple days. I worry about him in his toxic water.

•

Back at the Packard auto plant I stashed my bike over in the bushes by the neighboring cemetery. There was a guy there, standing in front of a grave, talking to it. I stared at him for a while, several minutes, before I snapped out of it and went inside the building.

My goal was to explore every single room in this massive structure. Up on the third floor, hanging out in a huge room that was nearly pitch-black—some sort of part had been fabricated here—I could hardly see or make out what was around me. I was taking a couple photographs of some abandoned boats and an RV of some kind, wondering how in the hell they got those up here, when I heard footsteps. *Not again.* I wondered when my luck would run out.

I completely froze while I listened. They were coming

from down the hallway, a group of them, heading toward me, and there were voices attached to the footsteps, male voices. Slowly, gently, trying to make as little noise as possible, I walked over to the door at the end of the room so that I could look down the long hallway where the footsteps were coming from, then I turned the corner, and there they were.

There were four of them. The closest one to me freaked out, and screamed. Literally, he jumped five feet back like a cartoon character. I apologized for startling them like that. I said hello and asked what they were up to, though I could tell by the way they dressed—with full backpacks, and spray-paint cans rattling—that they were graffiti artists. All were in their early twenties and turned out to be from Hamtramck, which isn't too far from here.

When I asked if it was cool for me to tag along with them to see what they were up to, they said sure, no prob. While we were walking down the hallway, which went on for days, the one kid I'd freaked out the most looked around. He asked if I was here all by myself, in a tone as if to say, Are you fucking crazy? I told him yeah, that I was alone, and that I liked hanging out in these buildings alone. It was peaceful and, I don't know, somewhat relaxing. Not quite sure if he believed me, or if he thought I was a liar and just saying that because I was a loser with no friends. I asked if they came across a lot of people hanging out in these buildings. While walking together they tell me they do, but usually other graffiti artists.

When I asked if it was safe going inside these buildings,

a kid who had said earlier that he was a graphic design student told me that he had actually been robbed once in this very building.

"Yeah, at gunpoint. By another graffiti artist! He pulled out a gun and stole all my paint. Didn't take my wallet, money, or anything, all he wanted was my paint. I even had an expensive camera in my backpack, but he didn't want it."

What a pussy. Not the guy who got robbed, but the guy who did the robbing. This kid was totally harmless, weighed about a buck and a quarter, and his fellow artist robbed him for his fucking paint? It's, like, get a fucking job at McDonald's and go buy your own paint, you know?

He went on to tell me that I had to be careful of other graffiti artists. Some of them were total dicks who would either tell you to get the fuck away from them or try to rob you. He told me that I got lucky, that he and his friends weren't like that. They just came into these buildings to do their thing.

While I was talking to him, I overheard the other guys in conversation. One of them was asking the other if he'd ever heard of the artist Jean-Michel Basquiat. I butted into their conversation by pulling out my iPhone and showing them my Basquiat screen saver. I was slightly embarrassed, since I didn't want to come across as the old thirty-something with no friends who was trying to impress them. As I was telling them the little bit I know about Basquiat, basically shit you could pull up on Wikipedia, like a pretentious asshole in a white-walled art gallery, I realized that these abandoned buildings are like contemporary art museums you can enter free of charge, that every day is a free day just as long as you're not worried about asbestos, or getting robbed at gunpoint by the artist who's "showing" up on the third floor.

On the roof there was a huge water tower that stood a good couple hundred feet up in the air, as well as a couple large trees. The view of Detroit was spectacular. The sun was out, and you could see for miles in all directions. Two of the guys have found a wall to paint; setting their backpacks on the ground they went to work. I looked down and could see two photographers a level below us taking pictures of the walls. They looked like professionals, with fancy gear and equipment. Not only that, they looked to be around my age. I went down to talk with them.

I also had a camera on my neck, which made me feel confident in approaching them. Like, *Hey guys, I'm just like you! I'm taking pictures too! Isn't this fun! Let's hang!* I guess I was hoping to make friends.

The photographers were both from Los Angeles and flew out to Detroit here just to do this. They'd been going around all over the city all weekend, going into all the buildings and structures, taking photos. They did this as a hobby.

One of them told me this was the easiest place so far to get inside, and that the others they had to kind of sneak in. He looked around at everything and then said, "It's like a bomb went off here."

And that was pretty much it. They didn't seem too interested in chatting or hanging out with me any longer—they were busy taking photos. I started getting neurotic, thinking that these were the cool kids and I was the nerdy dork with no friends; so I thanked them and excused myself.

I went back up onto the roof, where two of the four graffiti artists were hard at work spray-painting a wall. The other two were doing what I was doing—just kicking back, sitting against the edge of the roof watching the writers, enjoying the glory of the day. A couple minutes later the two photographers from L.A. came up and sat next to us. The one photographer opened up his camera bag and offered me half of his granola bar, which I accepted and thanked him for.

While watching one of the guys paint, I asked one of the L.A. photographers whether a lot of photographers came here to shoot urban decay. "Oh, yeah," he said. "It's Disneyland here. This is the number-one place in the U.S. to come for urban photography now.

"What's more trendy is sticking a naked chick in the middle of this."

"I've heard about that," I said, "I read an article once about this girl in New York who does that, I think her name's Miru Kim?"

"She's a goddess. She's awesome. No, she's great, but what I'm talking about is people who are just copying each other, just people who want to get into fashion photography. Their thing is shooting tied-up girls in urban settings."

I asked where they were planning to go next, and he told me they were thinking about going to an abandoned mining town in the San Bernardino area back in California.

"Have you been to the Michigan Grand Central Station yet?" he asked.

I told him that I'd tried to get into that building, but there was a police car parked in the post office parking lot next door watching the location like a hawk, so I wasn't able to hop the fence to get in. He told me that he and his buddy got into that building the other day.

"You got in?!"

"Yeah, we got in. I guess we got lucky. We ran into some guys there and they were saying Canada railroad cops patrol it, and they'll arrest you on the spot. But on the side of the building—you know how the road goes underground?—there's a section right there that's not boarded up, and you go underground basically, and you come out in the building. The guys there told us about a tunnel that could get us inside the book depository across the street, so we went underground to the book depository, too. There's a conveyor belt from when they used to load supplies from the third floor and convey them down to trucks, so we actually climbed up the belt and that was the most interesting part. Inside there are hundreds of thousands of books that are just sitting there disintegrating."

•

I spent the rest of the day pedaling around East Detroit. I came across a street in the middle of the 'hood that had been converted into folk art with a strong Basquiat influence. A whole street converted to a work of art, a gallery. And white people were parking their cars, getting out and walking around to look at it.

I came across a black guy who was about to walk into a house on the street, and asked if he was the artist, which he was. I asked if it'd be cool to chat with him. He told me sure thing, just give him a couple minutes, and he went inside his house and turned on some classical music. I walked around, taking pictures, and ten minutes later he returned. I said hello and told him what I was up to, that I was a writer traveling across the country talking to people, and I told him that he had a very interesting thing going on here, and I'd like to talk to him about it.

He looked at me with a flat expression. "I don't know who you are," he said.

That's funny, I want to say, neither do I. Not quite sure how to respond, I said hello and told him my name, and he said, "Well, I don't know who that is."

"Most don't," I said.

He told me if I wanted to talk to him, I first needed to make arrangements. "Call my office," is what he said.

I just stared at him. Was he serious? He was standing right here. And not only that, he had me wait around for ten fucking minutes so he could tell me *that*?

He then asked me if I wanted that number.

I told him, "No, thanks," and while I was walking away, my back turned, he said, "Have a great day."

CHAPTER FIFTEEN

Ignoring All Legal Disclaimers

*"Few buildings are vast enough to hold the sound
of time. Men came and went, they passed and
vanished, and all were moving through the
moments of their lives to death."*

THOMAS WOLFE

Outside the hotel Mrs. Harrington was surrounded by gardening equipment and a shopping cart full of plants. I asked her how it was going, and she told me that today they were going to plant a bunch of flowers in front of the hotel, make it more beautiful. I looked at the flowers, smiled, and since winter was coming I asked her about that, if the plants could survive, and she told me not to worry, everything they were putting in could survive winter. I like Mrs. Harrington—she gives me hope. Here is a lady who cares about her building, and Detroit, enough to plant flowers.

When I got in my car, I fired it up, pulled out of the garage, and drove to Grand Central Station.

On the weekends there was always a group of photographers, both professional and amateur, hanging around outside the Michigan Grand Central Station building taking pictures. I waited for that to pass, it now being Monday, since during the workweek a lot less of them show up. I drove a couple laps around the station in the '64, checking it out to see if any police officers were in the area. A steel chain-link fence ran all around the building, with barbed wire all along the top of it, and every couple feet metal signs warned "No Trespassing," "Private Property," and "Violators Will Be Prosecuted." One of these signs of course had the words "Fuck You" spray-painted onto it, and since I didn't see any security out here today, I parked my vehicle a couple blocks away, locked the door, and started walking toward the tall, ominous building.

Following the instructions of the photographer I had met at the Packard auto plant, sure enough, in the structure located behind the station, underneath the train tracks, I found an opening to get inside. Once you set foot inside, it only takes a couple of steps before it's pitch-black and near zero visibility all around you, except for the light coming way down on the other side, in the corner, a good forty or fifty yards away. I recommend bringing a flashlight if you choose to do this, because for many steps you have no idea at all what in the hell you're stepping on. While walking, I nearly stepped in a hole that was God knows how deep and would have found out just how deep if it wasn't for the sheet of plywood somebody had kindly placed on top of it.

I continued walking toward the light, and once I got there, I let my pupils get back to normal. Sure enough, I was "inside the wire," the wire being the fence that went all around the building, with barbed wire strung all along the top of it. From there I walked up and, just like that, entered the station.

•

I walked inside with no problem whatsoever, just as thousands and thousands of people once did. The station was built in 1913 and at the time was the tallest train station in the world. The tallest rail station in the world today is in Japan.

Inside and out the station is what's called Beaux Arts architecture. I Googled and Wiki'd all this shit, so don't think I'm an expert or know what the fuck I'm talking about, I don't. Once I walked into the pedimented door on the side of the building, I entered this grand space, with huge columns that go straight up to the ceiling high above. The walls were heavily graffitied, and there were arched windows, like windows in an old church, most of which were shattered but still allowed light to come in. It was completely empty. Nobody was there—at least I didn't think anybody else was inside the building—and I walked around for a bit with my camera, exploring while taking pictures. I felt relaxed, the only sounds being a car every now and then driving by, my footsteps, and the sound of my camera shutter bouncing off all the walls around me every time I took a snapshot. This building was designed by the same people who designed New York's Grand Central Terminal. It was 500,000 square feet, and I wanted to explore every single foot of it while it was still alive, while it was still standing, breathing, with a faint pulse. While walking around, I started thinking, Why in the hell, or how in the hell, did they allow this building to get like this?

The first floor was massive. I started wondering what you could do with this space. After walking around for a while, exploring and taking pictures, I came across a stairway that took you all the way up to the top floor. Once there, I migrated over to a window, or what once was a glass window. I was pretty high up, eighteen stories. I looked straight down, a long way down, and I thought to myself, It's that easy. All I gotta do is jump, and it'll all be over. Just like that, the end. I looked up and stared out onto Detroit, all the streets and neighborhoods. You could see all of downtown Detroit from the top floor, with the ugly-ass GM Building sticking up. Then I noticed that on the top floor of this building, where I was now, somebody had painted SAVE THE DEPOT in all caps, using red and white paint, all along the exterior. I started thinking about my son, and I got sad thinking about how in April 2009, about the same time he was born, the Detroit City Council had voted to have the building demolished, "passing a resolution that calls for expedited demolition."

•

The coolest thing about entering these old buildings is the picture they paint of how we used to think. While exploring, you can't help but stand in awe, taking it all in and wondering why in the hell we don't build, or think, like this anymore.

My son will never experience what it was like to be inside this building and if we keep on demolishing buildings like the one I was inside now, more than likely to make room for more condos and more surface-level parking spaces, since God knows we need more of those, he'll probably never get to experience these windows into our past for himself. We once thought big and put thought, design, and art into what we did.

It's disheartening to imagine my son one day exploring old abandoned buildings, and instead of being in awe like I was inside all these structures in Detroit, wondering, What in the hell were these people thinking? Instead of structures like the one I was in now, he could very well be going into a shopping mall, since all those are now closing down and being boarded up one by one across our country for various reasons. The buildings we build now are done pretty much the same way as our clothes, made the cheapest way possible. The flannel shirt I'm wearing now was made in 1961. I know this for a fact because it has the year printed on the inside tag. I purchased it in a thrift store for less than ten dollars; it's crisp, and the colors are bright, and it looks pretty much exactly the same as it probably did when it was first made half a century ago. Do you think the clothes being made now are going to last that long? No way. They all fall apart after the first wash and lose their color, fading almost as soon as you take them off the rack. By the time my son's my age, it's unlikely he's going to be able to go to a thrift store and come across an article of clothing made today. I can see him asking one day, "Dad, what's vintage?"

I wonder if, like Tower Records, antique stores will be extinct one day.

•

A few days later, as I was exiting the hotel lobby, a mob of people who lived in my building were all coming in, holding multiple bags filled with produce. Mrs. Harrington was holding the door for them. They seemed thrilled, so I asked what was going on. She told me that today was the East Side Market, and I should go down there, since there was also a beer festival going on. She suggested I go back inside and put on a heavier jacket, since it was a bit chilly out, and she felt that what I was wearing—Dickies, flannel, beanie—wasn't adequate for the conditions. As she held the door open for some lady carrying four bags of produce, she asked her how the market was. "Great," the lady said. "And they take food stamps!"

When I went to start my car so that I could drive to the market, of course it decided not to cooperate. I set off on foot.

•

Not far from the market was another series of abandoned buildings, so of course I had to check them out. Quickly I came across a couple individuals enjoying life, liberty, and the pursuit of happiness, casually smoking crack cocaine this glorious Sunday afternoon. Then I saw a white guy with a beard and a steel rod, sifting through everything on the ground. I walked over and asked what's up, and he told me that he was just looking for metal, which he called "punk metal." He collects pieces of punk metal in his side bag, which he then brings home, melts down with a torch, converts into fashion accessories.

I asked if he knew of more buildings like the one we were standing in front of. He rolled his eyes and said, "Go down to where you see Zimmerman's pawn shop over on the left, and it's the street behind that, the whole row of buildings—four or five in a row—is falling apart, and the whole neighborhood is crackheads and whores."

"Really? How do I get there?"

"I'll show you. Follow me."

Enjoying the fact that I was hanging out with a craftsman, I happily listened as he narrated Detroit for me as we walked.

"This is the beginning of the end," he said.

"How so?"

He tells me that Western civilization is declining. That the traditional values that have brought us to the pinnacle of world dominance are being given up. People no longer believe in God, that the people who believe in God are more steadfast fighters in what they believe in, since they think they'll be rewarded after death. "That's why we're headed toward communism," he tells me.

At this time in American history, the words *hope* and *change* were two buzzwords heard across the media and the country. While I was on the road, two words I heard everywhere I went were *socialism* and *communism*. Americans seemed to be afraid we're all headed in that direction.

I wasn't quite sure yet if this man was crazy or not, but I wanted to find out, so we walked on.

I quickly got the impression that he was a bit of a misanthrope as he went on about how they're pulling machines out of their factories and shipping them over to China, and how they have a shrinking tax base, and how sarcastically wonderful it was that they're now filming movies here in Detroit. And how our economy will now be based on importing garbage from Canada and burying it.

I noticed that most of the people on the street that we'd turned onto were black. He told me that we were headed for the black part of town, and released a subtle growl of disgust.

"Frankly, most people think I'm a racist—"

"How so?"

Casually he tells me that the Negro never achieved anything or has contributed anything toward civilization. That they've all given in to narcissistic self-indulgence.

I can't imagine why people would think he's racist. Okay, this guy was crazy. As I was thinking of the many counterpoints to his argument, he brought up hip-hop and asked me who in the hell was the genius who invented hip-hop. Good question. As I was about to try and find out via my Wiki app on my iPhone he went on to say, "You know, another way not to have a job, not to be responsible, just be a hoodlum with your pants hanging down to here so that you can hardly walk. . . ."

We all know how well regarded rock-and-roll was when it first showed up, a regular jobs program for white youth. I didn't agree with any of what he was saying, but I had to respect the fact that he was talking so openly about it to me. I'm sure most people who think that way keep their corrosive thoughts to themselves, or stay among like-minded folks.

"You know anything about evolution?"

"No," I tell him. "Not at all."

"Okay, so I won't even go there, then."

We stopped at the street corner. He pointed out the devastation—the bakery, the cellular phone store,

everything, all depressingly torn up and vacant. He
warned me to be careful. Before we parted ways, he asked
me if I was from America. Interesting question. When I
told him that I was, that I was American and that I was
from San Francisco, actually, I jokingly add that to many,
I guessed, San Francisco would be considered another
country. He growled back, "Ain't that right," and said
some comment about how that city should be wiped off
the face of the fucking earth. Kind of like Detroit, some
might argue.

Of course, as soon as he walked away, a day-shift street
hooker came up asking for a light. When I'd lit her cigarette, she asked me if I needed anything. I told her no, I
was fine, thank you, and continued on my way.

.

After walking around the neighborhood for a couple hours,
I noticed a cab parked on a side street lined with diseased
buildings. A couple seconds later this white guy came
strutting out from the alley behind one building, making
his way to the cab. He had on leather cowboy boots with
shiny steel tips, black jeans, a brown leather coat, cool Ray-
Bans, and his hair wasn't really a mullet, but it kind of
was—you could tell he took a blow-dryer to it. And the way
he was strutting back to his cab, chest out, looking around,
I could totally see this guy doing his hair in the morning,
looking at himself in the mirror, complimenting himself
on how awesome he and his hair looked together. This guy
just screamed self-confidence, and I knew right when I saw
him that I wanted to ride with him, so I went and asked if
he was working. He said that he was. "Jump in," he said.

So I did, and had to think for a second where I wanted to go, since I really didn't need a cab. I couldn't think of anything, because I had pretty much hit up all the neighborhoods and streets of inner-city Detroit, but just in case I hadn't, I asked him where the bad part of town was so that he could take me to the heart of it, please. He paused for a second, thinking deeply about that while slowly looking around. When he realized the answer to that question, it was like he got zapped with a jolt of electricity. He blurted out, "It's here!!!"

Well, that didn't help me, as I was thinking about somewhere else he possibly could take me to. He surveyed me from his rearview mirror and asked, "Where in the hell are you from?" So I told him. Since I couldn't think of anywhere to go, I just told him to take me back to my hotel. He turned the meter on and started driving.

"San Francisco, huh? Oh, I see, you're Chinese."

I corrected him by telling him I'm Korean. He told me that he guessed close, and asked, "Isn't Korea close to China?"

This was an interesting question. At least he didn't ask me what part of Korea I was from, north or south? I fucking hate that question and the types of people who ask me that. Relieved that wasn't the case, I told him, Yeah, Korea is close to China.

"Are they friends with each other?"

Who's not friends with China? I didn't know the answer to this one, so I told him, "About as good as friends with them as we are, probably."

He nodded. This guy had a really thick accent, sounded a bit Guido, and if I didn't know any better I'd say it was a Chicago accent. He told me, "I'm from Poletown."

Pole, I'm assuming, is Polish. Instead of asking whether Poland is good friends with Russia, since I really don't care, I asked him what he was doing, parked over by those abandoned buildings. He told me that he had to take a piss. That was all.

Wondering if he drove all the way to east Detroit to take a piss on it, I asked.

"No!" he exclaimed, and said that there was more to it than that. He was an artist and he had to go and borrow some money over at the pawn shop, see some things so he could buy some art supplies. His favorite thing to paint was people—there's nothing more interesting to paint, you know, the human figure, he said.

The guy had it made in my book. I could see myself driving a cab here in Detroit, make some money, dress however the fuck I want to dress, focus on my art when I'm not driving around Detroit, piss in old buildings, hang out in pawn shops. Jesus Christ, I should have fucking moved here years ago. I'm such a fool. Wondering what it was like being a cab driver here in Detroit, since I now wanted to be one, I asked him about it.

He told me that he actually worked another job as well, didn't say what exactly that other job was or provide any details other than to say that he more or less got laid off from that job—"that's a long story"—but thanks to his cab he stayed out of debt and the necessities and essentials were taken care of somewhat efficiently. As far as any big money left over after essentials and expenses were paid, there wasn't much of that. "You know, rent, food, clothes, electricity, that's all taken care of. As far as putting money in the bank? No."

He was quiet for a minute. Driving a cab was not for everybody, he told me, and he actually got shot at once, and hoped that didn't ever happen again; he tried to stay out of bad neighborhoods at night. "Stay out of the ghetto neighborhoods when it gets dark and you're fine." The cab company he drove for, he told me, was one of the biggest in the country; they had cabs in every state in America. If that was the case, why didn't he leave and go drive a cab somewhere else? When I asked if he'd ever thought about leaving Detroit he sighed and told me that he was forty years old. When he was twenty he wandered all over the world, but now felt he couldn't do that anymore. When he was twenty he went to San Francisco, Los Angeles, San Diego, Las Vegas, Arizona, Indiana, Missouri, New York, Virginia Beach, Ohio, Canada and "... uh, Idaho." He'd been all over, but when you get to be forty years old, he told me, your wandering days were more or less over. "I've already seen what I did, you know?"

"Yeah," I told him.

When we got closer to my hotel, I asked him if he liked it here in Detroit.

"Yeah, we got some beautiful girls here, I got a little bit of money, you know, I'm living the simple life, you know. I'm an artist, I drive a cab, got a roof over my head, food in the ice box, some scratch in my pocket, my studio for my artwork, and that fucking whore in my bed. You know what I mean?"

I do, and when he dropped me off, I tell him to keep the change, and he tells me to be careful down here at night.

I thank him for that and after watching him drive off I went back to my room, back to my simple life.

CHAPTER SIXTEEN

Sunday Stripper

"The most effective way to do it, is to do it."

AMELIA EARHART

I decided to check out the strip club on the corner over by Greektown. Not because I was bored, which I was, but for research purposes. That and it was Sunday. Six-dollar cover, three-dollar mandatory coat check. Not bad, except they rape you at the bar. In the land of Hamm's, seven dollars for a bottled beer. The place was dead.

Why was I at a strip club? I was on the road, that's why. Duh. Let me justify my decision to go to one by stating that it's what people do when they're on the road. I found this out back in Cheyenne. One of the guys I worked with doing day labor travels state to state working jobs while living out of motels. He told me one time that when he's on the road, there's nothing to do but drink and hit up strip clubs.

Only about half a dozen men—most were probably like myself, married and here on business. The brunette working the pole up onstage was wearing nothing but a black G-string and ten-inch platforms. From the bar I watched her dance for a bit while drinking my beer slowly. I looked around; everybody looked depressed. The guys were just sitting there silently, also drinking their beers slowly. I noticed everybody was kind of holding on to their money, holding on to what they had. I didn't see any money changing hands; nobody was throwing dollar bills at the girls or ordering beers one right after another, and the girls looked like models for a before picture for antidepressant medication. They all looked subdued, bored and distant.

The dirty-blond stripper down at the end of the bar was drinking a stiff drink all by herself, slowly, cradling the drink with one hand and smoking a cigarette with the other. Every time she took a drag, she'd inhale deeply and just stare straight ahead as she exhaled. It was like they all had given up on trying to get money from the men, and the men had given up on giving a shit. It was a standoff.

She had this vibe coming from her that she was probably thinking something along the lines of: There's gotta be more to life than this. This was depressing, and though at times I think I kind of like being depressed, this was a bit much for even me. That and seven dollars a beer was way too much. I'd started to think about going somewhere else when the brunette that had been dancing onstage when I first came in walked offstage and immediately walked over to me. I wondered what was wrong. This would be the first time ever that the hottest stripper would come up to me first—usually they don't, usually it's the busted-ass skanks that need rent money that come up and ask me if I want a dance. And usually what happens is the girl will walk over, introduce herself, maybe, depending how busy or how bored she is, chat for a bit, then ask me for my wallet, or ask if I want a dance. So I was prepared for all this when she came over and asked me how I was doing. I told her fine, expecting what would follow would be, Would you like a dance? But instead she sits next to me and immediately started talking about tattoos.

After mentioning that she liked my tattoos, she told me that she grew up out here, but lived in Vegas for six years and just moved back two months ago. From living in Sin City, she told me, she could tell that I was from the West Coast as soon as I walked in the door because I have "rocka-billy" tattoos, and that she'd hardly seen anybody here with that style. Out here, she told me that they have the tackiest tattoos she'd ever seen. Rolling her eyes she brought up a woman she saw out here once who had a tattoo on her neck of a hunting dog with a dead pheasant in his mouth. "I was like, Really? You put that on your neck?" She appreciated old-school tattoos, like the ones I have. "I think it's so hot."

"Thank you."

Obviously this girl had great taste, which made me wonder why she moved back here.

"If you don't mind me asking, why'd you move back to Detroit when things are so bad here?"

"Long story short," she told me, "I'm not going to give you a sob story," but both her grandparents are in hos-pice, so instead of going back and forth every two weeks she decided to move back into Mom and Dad's for a year and hang out here, and "get back together with all my old friends, you know?"

I asked her about the clientele that she had here, and she told me that this strip club was very event-driven, and when there was a sporting event downtown, people would usually come in. Watch a game, drink some beers, and then go see some tits and ass afterward.

She went on to tell me that she'd been stripping off and on for the last four years; she started in Vegas, where she worked as an event coordinator specializing in retail events but danced on the side and made some pretty good money doing both. When she moved back here, she tried to do what she was doing out in Vegas, but nobody wanted to hire her.

"Nobody here wants to pay me for anything," she told me, which is why she was now stripping for tips. In Vegas, the lowest-wage salary she had was sixty grand plus commission, plus bonus if the events went well, and out here in Detroit they're only going to pay a third of that. "Like, I've got friends who are well-educated, well-rounded, smart people, who graduated from college," she told me, "that are living back at home because they can't find jobs. They're delivering pizzas. It's crazy in Michigan."

I wondered if more women were getting into stripping since the economy was so shitty.

She told me yes and since she'd only just started working here, that this particular club used to have eighty-something girls on its roster. Now there's only forty-five. A lot of the girls who dance or strip here, she tells me, don't want to have a conversation with someone. If you notice when you go to a strip club, a lot of girls will go up to every single guy and ask, Do you want a dance? Do you want a dance? My name's so-and-so, do you want a dance? Here in downtown Detroit, there's not a lot of people to do that to, so the men go to other strip clubs. Like around Eight Mile. "But I like to talk to people," she says, "so I don't have a problem with talking to somebody all night."

If she could make more money north of Eight Mile, what was she doing here south of Eight Mile, I asked.

She released a sigh, rolled her eyes and said, "Well, nobody knows that I do this." All the people that she went to high school with were still around, and her parents, who never came downtown, "they think I'm a janitor." Intrigued, I listened in as she told me that she'd rather have them think that she was a janitor who cleans offices at night than have them find out that she was a stripper. To pull this off, she researched the janitorial profession heavily beforehand, she went online and found an office-cleaning company, she knew their address, she knew where they were located, found out what buildings they cleaned and that they went to work anywhere between six and nine p.m. and worked till late depending on how many buildings they had to close, and she even discovered how they had team leaders—what equipment they used and how to use it. She even went as far as to have T-shirts she silk-screened herself with their company's logo on them, so that when she left the house she was wearing that shirt and she exited with no makeup on. When she came back home every night it was always around the time when her parents were asleep. Proudly she told me that so far, they had no idea she was doing this, and that she was such a good bullshitter that when her parents asked about her job she'd complain all about it to them, "Oh, man, I hate my fucking job," and go on and on with these elaborate stories about how work last night "sucked" and how "Sam," who couldn't clean the floors properly was torturous to work with and how she had to redo cleaning the floors due to his incompetence as a janitor and again on and on about how she hated her job. "I've also found out online—both before and after taxes—how much they make per week, and I'll complain to my parents about that, too. I've got it down to a science!"

This girl was incredibly impressive.

We talked for a bit more, and not once did she ask me for a dance, though she did ask me if I wanted to do a shot with her, which I agreed to do and of course paid for. After that, it was her time to dance and she said she'd be right back, and when she excused herself, I watched her dance for a while on the pole while I finished my beer, and again I noticed that nobody was tipping, so I pulled five ones from outta my pocket and put them back into the economy, right there in her G-string. She gave me a hug, which I thanked her for. I then made my exit.

CHAPTER SEVENTEEN

Friendly Fire

"I am determined to sustain myself as long as possible and die like a soldier who never forgets what is due to his own honor and that of his country—Victory or Death."

WILLIAM BARRET TRAVIS

LT. COL. COMDT.

Letter from the Alamo

24 February 1836

After I paid for my omelet and coffee in the café downstairs, something happened that struck me as being kind of weird. I had paid for my meal and was leaving a couple bucks for the cook in the tip jar. Instead of saying, "Thank you," the cook asked me if he could borrow some money, that he'd pay me back. I'd never before eaten breakfast at a café where the person working the register asked if it'd be cool to borrow a couple bucks, so I was kind of thrown for a second by this request. I told him sorry, I didn't have any money to lend out, and left.

This made me not want to patronize the café anymore, but since it was Mrs. Harrington's café, and something I wanted to support, I shrugged it off.

While waiting for the elevator, I looked over at the front

desk, and for the first time it hit me that unlike every one of these kinds of hotels I'd seen across the country, especially here in Detroit, the Park Avenue Hotel doesn't do business behind bulletproof glass. Since Mrs. Harrington was in the lobby, I asked her about that. She defiantly said she refuses to have glass, and refuses to have a gun, and that the day where they had to put up bulletproof glass is the day she was out of here. "I will not capitulate to that kind of living. No way."

She felt this way even though her husband had been shot at once in this very lobby. The elevator door opened, but I ignored it. "What?!" I said. "Mr. Harrington has been shot at here?"

She then called her husband out of the back office to tell me about that time where he had to grab a gun from someone.

He told me that it was shortly before the Super Bowl in 2006, when the city was redoing the street out in front, and these two guys were pacing back and forth in front of the hotel, casing it in broad daylight, and finally they decided to storm into the lobby and rob it.

One of the guys was wielding a sawed-off rifle that he had stashed inside an umbrella, and the two of them had put stockings over their heads, and Mr. Harrington told me that there was all this screaming, "Mother fucker-this, I'll kill you-that," you know, and when he looked up he had a firearm pointed right in his face—

"And you grabbed it," says Mrs. Harrington.

"Well, not at first," says Mr. Harrington who explained that at first he just pushed it away . . .

Here, Mr. Harrington pauses, looks down in deep concentration, and tries to remember the sequence of confusing events. Mrs. Harrington looks bored and interrupts the silence, saying that he doesn't remember.

While being jabbed with the barrel of the gun—screaming and yelling—they ask Mr. Harrington for his money. So he opened up the drawer and there wasn't any money. So the one guy went ahead and just punched him, giving Mr. Harrington a bloody ear.

While he told me all this in detail—I got the impression that Mrs. Harrington thought her husband took way too long to tell his stories, because she had her elbow on the front desk and her head was now resting on her hand, and talking over him, she said, "You're losing half the story."

Mr. Harrington disregarded her comment and told me that when this happened he just got out of the hospital with a quadruple heart bypass and in situations such as this you think of all the things you're going to do—the first thing being "sticking your fingers in their eyes, you know, but you don't do anything." He just grabbed him and the two started wrestling.

The two of them ended up on the ground wrestling each other, and while that was going on the guy holding the gun was trying to shoot him but couldn't get a clean shot, and in the back room Mr. Harrington's son hears them thrashing around on the ground and comes out to see what's going on. The guy with the gun now fires off a round, but misses, and Mr. Harrington's son quickly manhandles the gun away from the guy, who takes off, leaving his friend on the ground wrestling around with Mr. Harrington. Finally that guy got himself untangled, and he took off running, too.

Mrs. Harrington was equal parts amused and exasperated. "Anyway," she said, with a slight smile, "they tried to shoot my husband, right here in this room."

CHAPTER EIGHTEEN

A Portrait of the Writer as a Young Artist

"All children are artists. The problem is how to remain an artist once he grows up."

PABLO PICASSO

When I typed the address into the search bar on Google I hoped that Google Maps would pop up so that I could get directions that way to the Harvest Festival, the party that Ika, the girl from the Ethiopian restaurant, had invited me to. Instead, what came up was a bunch of search listings for that address, and the very first listing on Google was a link to the financial history for the place. I really shouldn't have clicked on the link, because it really wasn't any of my business, but I did anyway.

PROPERTY FEATURES	FINANCIAL HISTORY
Single Family Residence	Last sold for $282 on
Year Built: 1913	5/30/2007
2 Bathrooms	Last assessed at $4,797 on
Approximately 1,736 Sq Ft	2008
Parking: Detached Garage	Previous sales
1 spaces	$282 on 5/30/2007
Lot size: 9,583.2 Sq Ft	Previous assessments
Stories: 2	$4,797 on 2008
County: Wayne	$4,797 on 2007
Heating type: Heating	$4,690 on 2006
Heating detail: Forced Air	
	Source: Public Records
Source: Public Records	

I then made the mistake of immediately calling my wife to ask if I could please have her permission to purchase a house here in Detroit somewhere near that location. I should have gone ahead and just done it. It's always better to ask forgiveness than to ask for permission, since word for word, her response was, *"Don't. You. Dare!* We are *not* moving to Detroit!"* She then reminded me that we have a son, and there's no way in hell she'd allow him to go to Detroit public schools. Head bowed in defeat, my white-picket-fence fantasy at the epicenter of America's greatness was unceremoniously shot down, and of course she was right. Detroit needs people moving in, not away, if it is to have any kind of chance. But your kid is your kid, and not some social experiment.

Something fundamental had shifted in her: she was a mother. My fatherhood, I guess, is lagging somewhat behind. Oh well.

•

The Harvest Festival was located deep in the heart of the East Side, and when I turned off Gratiot onto Mack on my bicycle, I pulled out my scrap paper from my pocket and looked around for a street called Elmwood. I couldn't find it.

On the corner where I was with my bike was a Marathon gas station with a Detroit Police car parked, door open. Two black police officers were standing outside the car. The one, a pretty big guy, was yelling at this young homeless-looking white guy for hanging out around the gas station and looking into other people's cars while they were trying to get gas. The cop told him several times that he couldn't do that and that he should get lost, which he reluctantly, did. When the police officer was done yelling, I approached him and asked if he knew where Elmwood was.

Without saying a word, he pointed me in the right direction and gave me this funny look. I could tell he was about to say something to me, but for whatever reason he chose not to. I thanked him, and as soon as I turned onto that street, *Do Not Enter* and *Wrong Way* started screaming in my head. I kept on pedaling. It was night, dark, and especially dark on this street; the streetlamps seemed not to shine as brightly around these parts. A stray dog walked by, groups of three or four kids with hooded sweatshirts stood on street corners, no cars were driving anywhere, many houses had all their lights off, then I saw the old abandoned brick schoolhouse she had mentioned.

I've been down many a street in my lifetime, both ones I should have gone down and ones where I shouldn't, both in this country and in others. At night, riding a single-gear vintage beach cruiser down a street where even in a car you'd be like, I ain't going down this street, fuck that, I'm turning around, I kept pedaling, slowly. Once I started getting closer to where the Harvest Festival was, just to make sure, I reached in my pocket to pull out my hand-drawn map, while three black guys my age were hanging out on a street corner, watching me. I looked down and saw I'd accidentally pulled a twenty-dollar bill out of my pocket instead of that piece of scrap paper with the map on it. God must hate me. My bad. I quickly shoved the twenty back into my pocket, pulled out my map, and found my way to Farnsworth Street perfectly fine, no problems.

Basically, the way to describe Farnsworth Street is that I felt like I had turned onto a street in the best part of Berkeley, California. The street was clean, all the houses were freshly painted and well kept, nice cars were all parked along the street—I couldn't believe it. The street had "NPR story" written all over it.

Stunned, I got off my bike and walked slowly up and down the street. I would totally live inside any of these houses, two-story, with front and back yards; one house even had an American flag posted on the outside of it, as well as a red Marine Corps flag. I've seen so many of these across the country, houses with both of these flags. It's like the guys who get out of the Marine Corps can't wait to purchase a house just so they can raise those flags.

·

When I got to her house, I saw she was dressed nicely. She told me that she had to run down to the store real quick but would be back soon. She told me to go around to all the other houses on the street, which had Christmas lights all around, that all the backyards were hooked together, so it was all one big backyard behind them. She told me of a house with a keg of beer at the back of it, so of course that was the house I went to first.

When I got there, a couple dozen kids were running around, playing with each other, half of them black, the other half white. Chairs were set up in a circle around a campfire, where people were seated, eating and drinking. The kids were going nuts waiting to go on the hayride— a guy driving up and down the street in a tractor with a trailer.

The back patio was where the keg was located—local brewery, of course—next to a table with a pitcher of sangria. Around the keg gathered a bunch of artist types, as well as some older-looking art teacher university professor types socializing with one another, everybody getting along, and this huge feast was going on inside the house.

As I walked inside, people were constantly coming in through the front door with food in their hands. There were various breads on the cutting board, dips, chili, soups, and other edible items on the dining table in the kitchen, and people were grabbing plates of food, standing around eating, complimenting the cooks, talking about how great this was, and how great that was, there were people drinking wine in the living room. I kept telling myself, Don't get drunk! Don't get drunk! Don't get drunk! over and over again as I picked up a red cup and made my way back over to the keg. I really didn't want to get drunk at all here, because I didn't want people the next day going, "Who in the hell was that idiot who got all wasted and drunk-drove the tractor all over the gardens ruining all the crops while singing 'Old McDonald Had a Farm'?"

"I know! What a fucking dick! I don't know who that idiot was, but I saw him throwing away his keg cups in the nonrecycling trash can. Asshole. We need to find out who invited this idiot and have a serious talk with that person. Somebody else told me they think he's the one who stole all the liquor from that one house across the street when he left."

I didn't want to make her look bad, since it was mighty kind of her to invite me here, a person she'd just met, so again I told myself over and over that tonight I was going to be on my best behavior and not get drunk.

I filled my cup, and after that I took a couple steps over to the side and just stood there for a bit, sipping my beer. I then sat and waited, hoping that somebody would come up and talk to me. Nobody did.

I sat there for a while, and I saw people walk in, and they said hello to the others, people they didn't know, and after a warm greeting would usually ask, So what do you do? I studied their body language: they'd lean in and listen, and once they were done, they'd reply by saying how interesting that was, comment, ask a couple questions, maybe even go so far as to say that they knew somebody or had a friend who did the same thing, and then the other person would comment back on what they did, and then they'd talk.

As I listened to their conversations, I noticed that a lot of them were using these huge long-ass words I'd never heard before; some people were wearing glasses, and they were talking about what wines go with what, installation art, documentaries that they saw on PBS, collective art galleries, experimental music, theater and screenwriting. I realized that these people were all highly educated, and I freaked out. I got all self-conscious and even checked to see if my fly was open. It wasn't, and I found myself drinking at an accelerated pace. Back at the keg, a girl my age then walked up, holding a red cup. She looked confused, and with a European accent asked me, "How do you do it?" I told her it was easy—grab the tap and pour into the cup—explaining that it was best to pour at an angle so you got less foam. She thanked me and walked away.

I went back to being a wallflower. I went from missing my wife and son to missing my mother. If she was here right now, she'd be pissed; she'd grab the red keg cup out of my hand, throw that away, tell me that I didn't need that, that I drink too much, nobody likes a drunk, and then smack the cigarette out of my mouth, ask for my pack so she could crumple that up, and with her Korean accent ask, "Why you standing there all by yourself in the corner? Why you slouching? Keep your back straight, head up! You always have your head down, what you looking for? Nothing down there, no good. Smile! You never smile, why you

never smile? Go, go talk to people, people are good, everybody here is having a good time, why not you? Go have
good time, talk to people, have fun, back straight, head up,
smile!"

•

I refilled my keg cup to the brim, corrected my posture,
and walked over to a bohemian-looking guy standing next
to another and said hello. He said hello back, and I asked
him if he lived here; he told me that he did, and quickly, I
don't know why, became uninterested and kind of walked
away. Perhaps he saw somebody more interesting to talk to.
I don't know. I drank more and edged over and talked to another guy; this one was a bit more chatty and talked to me
for a while. He also looked like an artist type—unkempt
hair, flannel, and jeans with paint smudges on them—and
I said hello and asked him if he lived here. He did, and he
asked me who I knew here, and I told him the long story
in a nutshell. He thought that was pretty cool—"She just
invited you here, just like that? Wow"—and then he asked,
"So, what do you do?"

What do I do? Jesus Christ, that's a good one. I told him,
"Oh, I'm a . . . artist." "Oh really? You're an artist?" "Um,
yeah." I couldn't believe I just fucking said that. Since it
seemed like everybody here was an artist, I guess I thought
I'd do the same. When I'm wasted and somebody asks me
that question, I'll sometimes tell them I'm an artist, and
whenever they ask what kind of art I do, I tell them that
I draw and then wait for them to say, "Oh you do, what do
you draw?" which I'll answer by saying, "I draw my own
path in life." But I wasn't that wasted, yet, so I went and

took a huge swig of beer from my red keg cup. I noticed that it was almost all gone, and I said, "I'm a writer slash photographer."

"What do you write about?"

Okay, obviously he didn't give a shit about my photography. That was another good question that he'd asked me, and I could feel myself breaking a sweat now. God, I wish I knew the answer to that one.

"I'm writing about traveling across the country right now, and uh"—since I didn't want to talk about writing, I switched the subject—"right now I'm going around documenting Detroit, doing a lot of urban decay kind of stuff, shooting black and white, you know, more dramatic, it really is like Disneyland out here for photographers."

"Oh, yeah, it really is here. You ever heard of Robert Frank?"

"Robert Frank? Oh yeah, he's amazing, love his work, very . . . inspirational."

I decided to change the subject once he started to ask me about darkroom techniques, so I asked how he liked living here, and he told me that he liked it a lot. "I was living in Portland, Oregon, for a summer, and I couldn't stand it over there."

"You couldn't stand Portland? Why not?"

I like Portland. Why didn't he like it there?

"Oh, I couldn't stand Portland. It's too comfortable. Everyone there is overeducated, unemployed, white, creative, and I just couldn't live there."

I nodded in agreement. Yes, this place, especially outside of this street that we're on, was definitely the opposite of Portland, definitely a lot more "edgy" and "real," out there like an episode of *Cops*. When I asked about personal safety, he told me, "You have to be careful, but for the most part, people here are really friendly. But we don't go out after dark, alone. Because I've had nothing but positive experiences here, I think I'm getting a bit stupider. Like, oh, those guys on the corner that are just staring me down, they like me, what up guys!"

I chuckled at that, and told him that I could relate, I felt the same way. We talked for a bit, and when I noticed that I was getting low on cigarettes, I asked if there was a liquor store anywhere close by, and he tells me of a corner store a couple blocks away that they all go to, but they always walk down there in pairs, never by themselves. "It's pretty shady."

"What would happen if I walked there by myself?"

"It would be . . . risky."

.

As I walked alone with my thoughts over to the corner store, I couldn't help but think, Okay, here you have this street that a bunch of people moved into, converting the street into something really great. They cleaned it up, they got gardens in their backyards, their houses are all extremely nice and well kept both inside and out, and I look at all the other houses on the streets in the surrounding area and wonder why the people who live on those streets don't do the same thing. Like they don't go, Hey, wait a minute, if they can do it, we can do it too!

I'm thinking maybe I should look into why that might be the case as I make my way inside the liquor store, which is pretty lively inside, with people purchasing both hard liquor and beer. The guy working behind the glass was Middle Eastern. I noticed that they also sold knit beanies, and since I had lost mine, I asked the guy if they had a black one. There was a bit of a language barrier going on between us, and when he pulled out the Obama beanie and asked me if I wanted that one, out loud, in a store full of at least half a dozen blacks wanting to get alcohol, in the 'hood, I said, "No, I don't want an Obama beanie!" in a way that was unintentionally rude. I paused because I hadn't realized what I'd just said and where I'd just said it until I did, and then I said, "I just want an all-black beanie with nothing on it. All black." He told me he didn't have any, so instead all I purchased was a pack of smokes. Returning to the Harvest Festival, I went back to the keg, filled up another red cup, and just hung out by myself, listening to the conversations going on all around me.

•

Bummed, I decided to leave. I walked over to her house; she was in the kitchen cooking, talking to a lady seated in a chair holding a baby, and I thanked her for inviting me, that I had a blast, everybody was cool, and just thank you. She said no problem, and even quickly introduced me to her friend, said I was a writer, and complimented my photographs of Detroit, telling her friend that even though the places that I'd taken pictures of had all been photographed a million times, the ones that I took were good. She told me to stop by anytime I wanted to and also stop by the Ethiopian restaurant before I left. I told her that I would, and then I grabbed my bike and pedaled around the neighborhood for a bit, since I was feeling a bit blue.

She was right: there was absolutely nothing original that I was doing, all my photos had been taken a million and one times before, I wasn't a photographer, and what about my writing? Was I saying or doing anything that hadn't already been done or said before, and done and said way better than I ever could or would? No. I wasn't an artist. I felt like a failed artist. All this made me want to cut my ear off and give it to one of the girls working on the corner of St. Aubin and East Warren. Feeling suicidal, since the thought of being shot didn't bother me as much as it had before, I pedaled around and took some more pictures of some more burned-down houses and a couple more interesting streets I really had no business going down, and then I pedaled back home, to the Park Avenue Hotel.

•

When I turned my bike back onto Gratiot, I came across that same homeless-looking white guy that the police officer earlier had been yelling at for peeking into people's cars at the gas station. He was back, and he looked about my age, walking aimlessly around the Marathon gas station again. I pedaled over to him to get his story, and since I was a bit drunk I started off by asking him what in the hell he was doing here, walking around East Detroit all by himself.

This guy was totally lost. I couldn't quite tell if he was mentally ill, or slightly drunk, or even both. I could barely make out what he was saying half the time, since his voice was also kind of soft, but when I asked what he was doing here, he slowly told me, "I'm fucked up, man. I just got out of the navy, and I ended up here."

Cars passed by us as he then asked me a question that I've asked many here, but hadn't been asked myself: "Do you like it down here in Detroit?"

"Yeah," I honestly told him, then I asked, "Do you?"

"No."

"Why not?"

"There's nothing to look forward to."

"How so?"

He then mumbled something, no idea what, totally inaudible. I even asked him a couple times to repeat himself, and I couldn't for the life of me figure out what in the hell he was trying to say until he said something else: "You got fifty cents, man?"

I told him no, I didn't have any change. Then I pedaled home.

•

When I got to my room, I opened up my door, walked in, poured myself a "glass" of wine from the box of red that I purchased at Walmart, into an empty Gatorade bottle, lit a smoke, turned the laptop on, listened to some Glenn Miller on iTunes, and sat down on the sofa. I could hear the cars tear by on the freeway next door. I looked up at the "Press On" quote that I'd found inside the old Packard auto plant a couple weeks back and still had hanging on my wall. I stared at that for a bit, and then I passed out and went to asleep.

I had to be out of town for a couple days for some college speaking thing I got invited to. I had a difficult time concentrating while I was away. My mind was on nothing but Detroit, and I couldn't wait to get back. When my plane landed back at the Detroit Metro Airport, I exited the baggage terminal, looking for a cab. Didn't see any, so I went up to the ground transportation area, where an angry lady was walking away, saying something about "Only in Detroit!" I didn't find out why she was so furious until I saw a guy wearing a trench coat standing there in front of the empty taxi stand. When I asked him where all the cabs were, he told me that there weren't any, and that my only option was to use his car service, which charged sixty dollars for a ride downtown. Something about a dispute between the city and the airport; they couldn't resolve it, so the city had kicked all the cabs out. Only in Detroit. Now *I'm* pissed. I explained to the guy that the city should be offering free shuttle buses for people who believe that there is still a functioning city to get to, that if anything, they should be paying people to come to their downtown. This no-cabs business was bullshit. The man in the trench coat agreed, but stood firm on his price. Just then, a five-foot-something Middle Eastern guy showed up and told me he could take me downtown for forty-five. So I jumped in his car.

He was from Yemen, and had worked a lot since he moved here, he told me. Once, on the freeway, he kind of drifted in and out of his lane a couple times, and he apologized and told me that he was extremely tired. He said that in addition to working all the time, he was also in school and studied all the time. The talking seemed to wake him up some, we made it safely to my neighborhood, and he dropped me off at the Park Avenue Hotel.

The next morning I came across Mrs. Harrington out-side the building tending to her plants. When she saw me, she stopped what she was doing to ask where in the hell I had been and what I was doing going off for a couple days like that.

"Don't ever do that again!" she said, in a tone of voice I had not heard from her before. She wore an expression that was part annoyance and part relief. She had been worried because I was going in and out of all these buildings all over Detroit all alone, and she had begun to think that something might have happened to me.

"What if something happened to you," she asked, "how will we know?"

What would it matter? I thought. I'd be dead.

"How will your wife know?"

I hadn't even thought about that one. She then made me write my wife's cell phone number down on a piece of paper and give it to her and the front desk guy in case something happened to me. I did and thanked her sincerely. "You have to let me know when you leave like that," she said. She paused, rubbed her dirty hands together, and her expression softened. "I was so worried."

I promised her that I would, and when I got in the elevator to go up to the third floor the guy who I was sharing the elevator with told me she was freaking out while I was away, telling everybody I was missing.

"I was just out of town for a couple days."

"That's what I told her, but she was all, No, he's missing!"

My mother used to always freak out if she didn't know where I was or hadn't heard from me. Sunday was the day where I was always supposed to make a phone call and check in with her to let her know I was alive, as well as tell her *never* when she asked me, again, when I was going to go back to school or, "When are you going to settle down and raise a family?"

If I didn't call on Sunday, she'd inevitably think I was dead, in jail, or kidnapped.

I've stayed at hotels such as this where they really don't give a fuck if the people who are staying there live or die. Sometimes, like the place I was staying in Denver, they kept in the lobby several garbage bags completely filled with clothes left behind from somebody who just left without saying good-bye.

This place, the Park Avenue Hotel, is feeling a lot like home to me, and it's making Detroit feel like home, as well. I'm even catching myself calling it home now when I talk to people. I have lived my life resisting such feelings—of acceptance, or belonging, or maybe what humans might even call *love*. But that's the feeling the Harringtons have made me feel, in spite of my very best efforts.

•

I decided to renew at the Park Avenue Hotel for another month. That month would pass in much the same way as the rest of my time in Detroit, and by the end of that month, I would begin to feel the pull of my other "home"—and wife, and child—with both anticipation and dread.

Soon would be my moment of truth, and I'd been fantasizing about walking down to my bar on the other side of the freeway—the one where the bartender knew me and most evenings plied us both with shots; often he was more plastered than I was—and stepping inside the door, seeing Kerouac seated all by himself down at the end of the bar. At the beginning of this road trip of mine I probably wouldn't have said anything to him. I don't know him and I really wasn't that kind of guy. But now that I'd gotten a taste of what it was like to be on the road, I'd probably take a seat right next to him, order a shot of whiskey and a beer, slam my shot, and once my beer was mostly gone, I'd look over and if he wasn't too drunk and would listen, I'd say hello. I'd pretend I didn't know who he was and tell him all about how I left my wife and son to hit the road. He would have said he knows exactly what that's like, that he himself has spent a fair amount of time at large in America. Only then would I ask him for advice.

If he were me, I'd ask him, would he go home or keep on going? Now, this fantasy comes with full knowledge of how Jack himself answered the call of home and responsibility. He floored it and blew right through.

But, in my fantasy, he tells me to go back to San Francisco and look for a job. Which is ironic, I guess, because when I visited Kerouac's gravesite several years prior, I'd felt awkward, on the verge of giving up writing altogether, and I remember mentioning something to myself while standing over his grave about how I was going to give up writing and look for a regular job when I returned to San Francisco.

But before I left Detroit, there was something I wanted to do, and that was find a job here. Again, if you can dream it, you can *try* to achieve it. Nothing's going to stop you. Right?

CHAPTER NINETEEN

Failing Journalism 101:
A How-to Guide

*"I hate newspapermen. They come into camp and
pick up their camp rumors and print them as facts.
I regard them as spies, which, in truth, they are."*

WILLIAM TECUMSEH SHERMAN

Waking up at around noon, hung over, I turned my laptop
on to do a couple searches on "Time magazine Detroit
House." Armed with some intel, I exited the hotel lobby
with my bike. I've forgotten his name, since I'm terrible
at that, but the one guy with a white beard that's always
wearing the Tigers hat was outside watering the plants
around the hotel, and asked me what I was up to today, so I
told him I was just going to check out the *Time* magazine
house, and asked if he'd heard of it.

Time magazine is one of the largest circulating peri-
odicals in the country, and this year they'd bought a house
here in Detroit. Not a bad editorial decision. Since every
other industry here in this city is dying, why not have another one die here as well? Supposedly, the magazine is
sending their journalists to stay while they did stories on

Detroit. In one of their recent issues, they'd made a big deal out of this purchase.

"Oh, yeah," he says, "I heard they got people staying there and I saw something about it on *Good Morning America* or something, where's it at?"

"I think over by West Village or Indian Village. One of the two. I don't know exactly where it is yet, but I'm gonna find it."

He then gave me directions to those neighborhoods: "You go down quite a ways, and then you'll see signs that say Historic Indian Village, it's all beautiful mansions."

"Really? Is it a nice part of town?"

"It is but it isn't. It's a nice part of town that's right next to the bad part. Indian Village itself has beautiful homes, old homes, old-old homes—it's a pretty nice place, and right now it's a lot of young upbeat professionals, you know, doctors and lawyers. You know, young professionals that have bought the homes and restored them. There's still some old money in there, but it's mainly young folks, you know it's a ride, it'll take you a good forty-five minutes."

Ah, the Green Zone. Hopefully the neighborhood would have a new temporary resident. Me. I thanked him, and as I got on my bike he called out, "Good luck."

•

Pedaling along on my bike, I wondered to myself, "How does one write for *Time*?" I've read *Time* before, mostly while taking a shit, and it's like all those dorks in high school who wrote for the high school newspaper, all grew up, went to college, and got jobs at a magazine and pretty much continued writing the same bullshit articles they all wrote in high school, but at a much higher level. Circulation-wise, that is. Same kind of writing, really. "What's Wrong with Cafeteria Food, and What We Can Do to Make It Better!" or "An Inside Look at School Spirit: Why It Still Matters and How It's Changed (It's Not What You Think!)."

I thought about bringing a box of wine as a nice gesture, but chose not to. I'd have had to go all the way out to Walmart in Dearborn to purchase that, and since my car was still out of commission, parked in her parking lot over by the hotel, at least I hoped it was still parked there—I got to thinking that it would be a good idea for me to check up on it sometime soon.

For a split second the thought of printing out a couple writing samples so that I'd have something to show them crossed my mind—maybe I'd even print out a résumé and cover letter—but I chose not to do either, since that might be a waste of paper. Like *Time* would let me write for them. Instead, what I thought I would do was just step into character and tell them I'm a writer who just recently moved to the area, and it'd be cool to write an article for them in exchange for a place to crash. Stay at their house while I'm writing it. It'd be nice to sleep on a bed with an expensive mattress and be able to take hot showers in the morning.

While riding my bike, I thought about what I would do once I found the *Time* magazine Green Zone house. I'd done door-to-door sales before, and sucked at it; I wasn't ever good at selling anything, especially myself, and maybe that was my problem. Maybe I needed more confidence. Maybe instead of waiting for people to bang on my door for writing assignments, I needed to start banging on theirs.

Soon enough, after I'd passed by a couple run-down neighborhoods, just like that, like turning the page onto an entirely different book written by an entirely different author, *The People of the Abyss* by Jack London on to F. Scott Fitzgerald's *Great Gatsby*, I came across a street filled with houses straight out of an episode of *Lifestyles of the Rich and Famous*: *Detroit*, huge mansions, front and back yards, sprinkler systems, a BMW parked next to a Lexus, trees manicured, lawns freshly mowed, jars of Grey Poupon in the refrigerators.

It didn't take me long at all to spot the house that I thought was *Time*'s Green Zone house. It looked exactly like the photo I'd come across online. I stopped my bike in front and stared at it, and as I did, I was envisioning my 1964 Mercury Comet Caliente parked, dripping oil onto the driveway. I wanted to call that house home. I stared at all the other houses on the street while the smell of cut grass hit me and the sounds of peace and quiet, set to birds happily chirping, provided the sound track. I sighed as I imagined how wonderful it must be to write for *Time*. Lucky bastards. I hated them.

On that very same street was a white lady raking leaves and dumping them into a trash can. I approached her and asked, "Is that the *Time* magazine house?"

"I don't know if I should answer that."

Oh, really? I was thinking, since waterboarding is slightly illegal, to ask a couple of questions instead. I then relayed what I did know about the house: "Gray, six bedrooms, right?"

She appeared offended at the mention of six bedrooms and said four was more accurate.

Okay, cool. So I did have the right house. Now that I had the right house, I thought about coming back later on that night so I could egg it. Then I remembered there was no grocery store over by where I lived, so I couldn't do that, but I could sure as hell teepee it. What am I, in junior high again? Snap out of it, Colby, I'm in my early thirties, I came here to knock on the door and see if I could write for them, not to vandalize the joint.

Feeling myself chickening out from knocking on their door, I asked if she lived on the street.

She informed me that she did. Then she released a laugh as she told me, "Why, do I look like hired help?"

Wow. She was white, so no, I didn't think she was hired help, nor was I in any way trying to insult her, no way. I could also tell that she was slightly kidding around, so I started asking her about the neighborhood, and we got to talking. She was friendly and told me of a restaurant nearby that was no longer there, where Henry Ford used to eat, how the old apartment buildings in the neighborhood had always been where a lot of reporters lived over the years, and how they first started building homes in their neighborhood in the 1800s.

She went on to tell me that a lot of young people had moved in, bought houses here and were redoing them. The young and the lucky. People my age buying property.

Maybe my mom was right. Maybe my problem was that I didn't think big, and instead of always finding the most depressingly cheapest possible place to live whenever I did something, I should be more like *Time*, think big, crash in the nice part of town, live here, live nice, and write about have-nots that way.

When I asked if they had a grocery store, she told me that they did have one close by. "You know what, it ain't great shakes, but we're all really happy it's there. We really are."

Now I was totally jealous. I should buy my eggs there, I thought. When I told her that I'd been staying downtown, and one of the frustrations with living down there was no grocery stores, she told me that was exactly what the article that the guy who's staying there now was about, about how there were no grocery stores and how there were hardly any chains anymore.

We chatted for a bit; she was a kind lady. I told her about the historic street I came across over by Wayne State and how when I spoke to that one lady, she told me that she'd had problems with people trying to break into their house, so I asked her if she'd had the same problem here.

She told me that they do because they view it as an affluent area, "yeah, they still kind of view this as kind of the place to go to shop."

"Shop?! Really?" I frantically looked around. "There's shops around here?"

"No," she told me, "I mean the free shopping, the breaking-in kind of shopping."

"Oh."

Since I didn't want to take too much of her time, I thanked her.

•

Hearing a lawn mower, I looked down the street to see where the noise was coming from, and I quickly pedaled over to the guy mowing. I didn't ask if he lived at the house where he was mowing, not because he was black—that's racist—but because I could see his white van parked in front of it. I asked if he was from Detroit, which he was. I made a comment about how nice this neighborhood was, and he told me that all the neighborhoods are nice. "A lot of times a lot of things happen from outside forces, not necessarily from the neighborhood."

When I asked him how the job market was here, he told me that it was lousy. If times got worse, I imagine that he'd be affected by it, since the less money people have, the less money people have to hire other people to mow their lawns. When I asked him, he told me yeah, it had affected him; that it's slowed it down a lot, as far as the economy goes, "the economy is lousy. I don't really worry about it because I know when things are good, it's good, and when things are bad, it's bad for me too. It's bad for all of us."

For now he told me that he got by. In regard to the

future? "My opinion is, it's going to get worse before it gets better, anyways."

·

I checked out the neighboring Indian Village, which was just as nice, after heading back downtown.

I wondered, now that I knew where to find the house, should I go back sometime and knock on the door? What if somebody was inside? What if it was an editor? What if he was kind and invited me inside, told me to take a seat on the sofa, asked me if I'd like anything to drink, like a glass of wine? I'd tell him kindly, "No, thank you, but a glass of ice water would be mighty nice. I don't think the sink water at my hotel is distilled and it tastes kind of funny whenever I drink it, kind of lead-y," and he'd be telling me that'd be no problem, he'd get me a glass of purified tap water, and once seated in the living room he'd excuse the noise that the hired help was making while they were mowing the lawns and gardening in the front yard. I'd tell him it was no big deal, nothing like the freeway that I lived next to. He'd then start off by asking me, "Why, how can we help you, Mr. . . . ?"

"Oh, yes, Buzzell. The last name is Buzzell."

He'd nod, while I could see the Rolodex in his head, frantically flipping through cards to see if he knows that name, and just before he figured out that he'd never heard of nor seen that name in any byline whatsoever, an editorial intern wearing an apron would appear. The apron looks familiar, it has the magazine's logo embroidered on it, I think it's one of those items they give away for free when you subscribe. I could also see that he's wearing a Columbia School of Journalism alumni sweater underneath, and in his hand is my glass of water. I'd gratefully thank him, but then shoot him a look. "What the fuck is this?" I'd yell. "I can't drink this!" I'd shove the glass back in his hands, spilling some of the water onto his apron, and tell him, "I said ice water!" He'd frantically apologize for his blunder multiple times, and quickly go back into the kitchen to get me some water with ice. I'd pretend not to be insulted and unfluster myself.

"I swear, these kids nowadays, full of entitlement and the-world-owes-me mindset, straight-out-of-journalism-school, fucking prima donna, spoon-in-their-mouths pansies! They can't do anything right."

The editor would smile while telling me that he likes my style. We'd then proceed to talk business.

"What can we do for you today, Mr. Buzzell?"

"Oh, yes, I want to write a piece for you guys."

"You do?"

"Yes. You know, there's been so much negative press lately in the media in regards to Detroit. . . ."

"Oh, we know."

"And nobody hurts quite like the poor. . . ."

"Oh, we know."

I notice a subtle erection forming from his tan pleated khakis as he folds his legs, and I continue.

"And I was thinking—"

Just then, Columbia shows up with my ice water. I rudely ask him, "Where the fuck is the sliced lemon?"

He quickly leaves the room again, and after convincing the editor that I am the guy they're looking for, and how I should write a positive uplifting piece for their publication on Detroit, focusing on all the good, and not the bad, we'd shake hands, and he'd tell me that I could move into their house the next weekend, and he is really looking forward to seeing my first draft in his in-box on Monday morning.

I'd pedal back as fast as I can to the Park Avenue Hotel, where I can act like a crazy who's just won the lottery and is going to spread the wealth and buy drinks for everyone until all the money is gone! Mrs. Harrington would be in the lobby when I got there, and I'd tell her that I did it! I got a gig writing for *Time*! She'd give me a hug: "I'm so proud of you! You did it!" and she'd tell me how great that news was, and while cracking open a bottle of champagne in the hotel lobby, passing it around to everybody coming in and out of the building, I'd tell her to put the word out to everyone and post flyers up in the elevator telling everybody that they're all invited to stay with me and party at the *Time* Green Zone house, that it's going to be a house party the entire time I'm there!

Mr. Harrington would step out from the back office with a phone in his hand, and he'd tell me that the call is for me, that it's Hollywood on the other line. I'd ask him to tell them to fuck off, which would cause the lobby to erupt in crazed cheers.

I should also contact the girl who invited me to the Harvest Festival, and tell her that I'm returning the favor, inviting her and her friends to my party, and how I think the theme should be "Rags to Riches," and for all to dress accordingly.

A female bartender who works at the Town Pump, the bar on the first floor of the Park Avenue Hotel, would walk gracefully into the lobby. She's the one that looks like a model from France and the same exact bartender who cut me off the night before. Her eyes would be fixated on me as she glided toward me in her high heels. I'm being congratulated by everyone in the building, receiving pats on the back, shaking hands, signing autographs, kissing babies, group photos taken on cell phone cams, etc. She'd have sex radiating from her as she walks up to me and seductively says, in her best Marilyn Monroe voice, that the word around the bar is that I got a writing gig for *Time*, that all her regulars were gossiping about that, and she was wondering if there was any truth to any of it. I'd tell her it was true, that I was going to write something for them, and she'd take off her shirt, she's wearing no bra underneath, her tits are perfect.

"Take me to your room and fuck me."

"What?!"

"I want to have your babies."

Oh, shit. That reminds me. I have to call my wife and tell her the good news as well. I'd then tell her, "Sorry, babe, I'm already taken," as she burst into tears and stormed off sobbing.

I then excuse myself from everyone and make my way up to my room. People are chanting my name over and over again, and I do the Joe Namath victory finger pointed skyward as I make my way into the elevator.

I also have to call up all my friends back home as well, all four of them, and tell them the good news, that I got a gig at *Time*, that I'll be staying at their house here in Detroit, and to all come and crash with me, that it's cool, a two-story, and bring whoever they wanted with them as well.

"Dude, you're staying at the *Time* magazine house and you're going to be throwing a party the entire time you're staying there? Don't you also have to write an article for them on Detroit or something to stay there? When are you going to find time to do that?"

"Oh, yeah, don't worry, I got that all under control. Check it out, the last time I was in China I met this guy, his name's Calvin, he showed me around for a bit and told me that he wanted to be a travel writer someday. We have been communicating ever since via email, so I let him know I got a gig for *Time* and asked him to write the article for me."

"What?! You got some guy in China to write the article for you?"

"Oh, yeah, so I can party, I'm totally outsourcing it, baby! Nothing's made in America anymore anyway, you know that. I'm paying him three cents a word. No idea how much rice that can get him, but he seemed happy about it and said that was cool. Told him to just Wiki Detroit, read about it, and then do a couple Google searches and just write something up, something positive, not negative, we always hear the bad, never the good."

"Oh, I know."

"Yeah, they want a two- to three-thousand-word article by Monday, they're paying me three dollars a word, I'm paying the guy in China three cents a word, it's perfect."

·

When I got back to the Park Avenue Hotel, Mrs. Harrington was in the lobby, and she asked me how it's going. Kind of depressed, I tell her fine, and I talk with her about staying here longer. I've been here in Detroit for a month now, and since I have to be in New York City in a couple days, I want to pay in advance for another month before I leave. She tells me that's no problem at all and even jokes about me staying here at the hotel forever and never going back home. I smile and joke back to her, who knows, that might be the case.

CHAPTER TWENTY

Love Thy Neighbor

"If you don't live it, it won't come out of your horn."

CHARLIE PARKER

After another night of heavy drinking at a dive over on the other side of the freeway, I woke up hung over and after a shower was all set to go. Instead of taking the elevator down I took the stairs. I saw that Mr. and Mrs. Harrington were seated at a table inside their café. The door was open, so I waved hello, and Mr. Harrington informed me that I just missed it, that the police were just here. When I asked what happened, Mrs. Harrington told me to take a seat, which I did.

She told me about a tenant who was moving out, and when she checked the room to make sure that all the belongings are still there, she saw in the closet her three-hundred-dollar vacuum for the tenants that has been lost now for several weeks, and it was under a coat. She took the coat off it and said, "You have my machine," and he said, "Oh, I didn't know it was there."

Mr. Harrington looks like he's been through this a million times before and calmly mentioned, "He also had the towels in his car."

"Oh, yeah!" she snapped. Later when the tenant comes downstairs, she gave him his hundred-dollar deposit back, and said, "Now, please leave the lobby." And it became really ugly. Everybody started screaming and yelling, she told me, and there was a scuffle, even spitting in the face. . . .

I should wake up earlier—the things I miss while sleeping in.

When the police came, they listened to all their stories, and there's confusion over the vacuum cleaner—specifically who owned it. The tenant moving out claimed he was given the vacuum, and when they started believing that scenario, Mrs. Harrington started raising her voice. "The police are now saying that we have given him the three-hundred-dollar vacuum cleaner. Yeah, just gave it to him, that's what he said and the police believed it!" So more police came— "to arrest me! *To arrest me!* I mean, this is why Detroit is dying, honey, it is in the grips of death. I said to the police that every place, every parking lot around here, used to be a building, and look, you've destroyed the city, but they are going to arrest *me?!* Well, let them arrest me! I was going to go to jail for that."

I like this lady a lot.

Frustrated, she explained that this is what they are up against, "this is why the city is dying, that's why we're the only ones standing. . . ."

She then was up and about, as the restless energy inside her often propels her from conversation to garden to paying proper attention to some tenant, back to conversation. Mr. Harrington is somewhat less active; and when she left, he told me a story meant to illustrate a recent decline in the neighborhood:

A guy from England had a bus ticket and got as far as Detroit before running out of money. Somehow he ended up at this hotel. From talking with him, Mr. Harrington realized this guy was a mental case. So he called the health clinic over at Wayne State, and told them he got this guy, a mental case who needs help, and that somebody should take him down there. But the guy wound up staying at their hotel for a couple weeks, and he would walk from here off to the hospital every day for his appointments. One day, he was crossing over the bridge, over the freeway here, "And there's this stocky black guy standing in the middle of the bridge who used to rob people all the time there, and so the black guy says to him, 'Stop, I want your money, your watch and wallet, or else I'll throw you off this bridge.'" The guy told him, "Pardon, what do you mean?" Mr. Harrington explained that he couldn't understand his accent, so he leaned over to him and said, "Pardon me, I don't understand," and the guy said, "Motherfucker, I want your money," and the guy said, "You want what?" Now the guy's shouting at him, but then he just tells him to go away. And when he walks in here, he says, "Mr. Harrington, there's a black folk at the bridge and he's saying terrible things. I think he's saying terrible things about my mother."

Mrs. Harrington is back now, and catches the tail end of his story, and must have heard the story a bunch of times before because she corrects her husband by saying, "You don't say it right, you screw up all the stories! He said, 'He said something *indecent* about my mother.'"

And then she says, "There is an exodus, a total exodus of people leaving. Everybody is leaving because they are being robbed in this neighborhood." And then, just like that, she excuses herself again from the table, saying, "I have work to do."

•

It seemed that the café might not make it. They couldn't find a reliable cook who didn't have creative differences with them, or hit up the tenants for money. I wondered what they were going to do with this space, and Mr. Harrington told me that the reason they started the café was because there wasn't any other place to get breakfast.

The idea was to get them to provide a very good inexpensive breakfast for everyone whose rent was paid up. If you're paid up, you'd get two eggs, hash browns, one sausage, or one piece of bacon. And toast. The breakfast and café was to create a lively place where people can interact with each other, livable for those here. And it makes the hotel more of a desirable place. Mr. Harrington told me that his wife creates an atmosphere in this place where she's got everybody laughing, everybody talking, that makes it a nicer place to live than someplace else where nobody even knows each other.

Just then, Mrs. Harrington, who was chatting with another person who lived in the building, peeked her head back into the café and asked Mr. Harrington about one of their tenants—if he's gay or not.

"Yes," her husband told her, "he is."

She asked, "He's in the closet?"

"Yes."

Mr. Harrington said that this particular person was a really nice guy, and Mrs. Harrington agreed but said, "A real sweetheart, but he brings those dirty cats in from Cass Corridor."

Mrs. Harrington then went back to her conversation, but peeked her head back into the café again and asked me if I'd like a piece of cake. I told her no, thanks, and like my mother, who would always ignore me when I told her that I wasn't hungry, she said, "I'll get you a piece of cake." She came in shortly after with a piece of pumpkin cake for me on a white plate, silver spoon. She asked if I wanted coffee, and before I could answer, she said, "I'll get you coffee."

With tenants coming and going, and the police action still heavy in the air, Mrs. Harrington whirling like a dervish, Mr. Harrington remained calm and collected. He was in the middle of telling me the story of the neighborhood when Mrs. Harrington dashed into the café again and asked her husband, "Why do you always talk? Why don't you ever let him talk?" and stepped back out.

Mr. Harrington ignored her, the same way my father used to ignore my mother whenever she would talk to him like that. Mr. Harrington continued. "So anyways, Tiller built this building, and 1929 came and he was wiped out, so there was a Jewish fellow who bought this—"

Just then Mrs. Harrington whirled into the café and excitedly told us what she'd just heard: "You know what I heard this morning? America is the most segregated country in the world, where everybody is in their own little corner, you know, and it is *so* the truth. I lived two doors away from a Jewish family but never knew they were Jewish . . . it just doesn't even register with me, okay? And—"

Mr. Harrington pleaded with her, "Can I just finish this story? *Please?*"

"Okay," Mrs. Harrington quickly snapped back to her husband. "But when I married you, I told you I did not want to live in Detroit!"

•

Only days later, there was another upsetting morning at the hotel.

I asked Mrs. Harrington what happened, and she told me they'd been suspecting that the guy running her café was stealing, and so she told her son and he installed a hidden video camera, and sure enough they found him stealing, so they fired him. Thus their café no longer had a cook, nor a person to operate it. Mrs. Harrington was so proud of her café, and now she seemed distressed.

This spurred another story of how she once got her back broken here in the very same lobby where Mr. Harrington got shot at. An abusive male relative of a tenant grabbed her and slammed her against the elevator.

I was starting to think that I wasn't sure if Detroit could survive without the Harringtons, but I was equally unsure that the Harringtons could survive Detroit. Right then, this black guy who lives on my floor walked into the lobby, and he heard us all talking about Mrs. Harrington writhing on the floor in pain and indignation, and told me that he remembered that day, and that when he walked into the lobby and saw her on the floor, "I just about cried." There were people in the lobby who witnessed all this go down, and he said to them, " 'Why y'all let this happen?' And everybody looking at each other just scratchin' they heads."

I told him it seemed that the cops treated them the same way, and he said, "She's very nice to everybody in here, she's not racist or none of that. How in the hell is she racist if eighty percent of the people in her building are black? She doesn't care what color you is, she just trying to be nice to everybody."

She heard this from him and thanked him by giving him a hug and a peck on the cheek.

"We come from the same people," she said quietly. "We're all the same."

The black guy then told her, "Me and you, we grew up in church." And then he pointed to me. "He didn't."

A look of shock appeared on her face as she asked if this was true, if I wasn't raised in church. I told her that it was true, and that my parents didn't raise me in a church.

"You don't believe in Jesus?"

"Umm . . ."

I hemmed and hawed, thinking about what to tell her. I didn't want to break this lady's heart by telling her no, I don't believe in God, it's a good story but I'm more of a nonfiction kind of guy. I flashed back to being at the hospital and my mother asking me if I believed in God, and I answered by telling her, "No, I don't," and it's bothered me ever since I said that to her. I think I should have told her yes to spare her feelings, because really, what does it matter?

Still in a state of shock, Mrs. Harrington then asked me again, with such searching in her eyes, "You do believe in God, right?"

"Umm . . ."

I was about to break into a sweat, squirming. Mr. Harrington could see where this was going, and he touched my arm and asked me if I'd like to go next door with him for a drink, which seemed like some sort of divine intervention. I of course told him I'd love to, and followed him outside. While standing outside for a second, he told me a little bit more about what happened with the guy running the café.

The guy lived in the building but never paid his rent, so Mr. Harrington had given him a notice of eviction, but the guy had appealed to Mrs. Harrington, and she had agreed to let him live in the building *rent-free* if he helped out in the café in the mornings, on account of his being a Christian.

"He gives my wife his bullshit, that he's Christian. All you have to do is cry or tell my wife you're Christian and you want to do better, and she'll bend over backward for you."

He told me that he confronted people like that all the time, but shouldn't have to. "I'm eighty years old," and the people are up to no good around here. They pick on old people and cripples and just beat the shit outta them and take everything they have. One of the things for Detroit to survive, he told me, is that it has to be safe; that this simple concept is such an important thing. He asked me why would somebody from the suburbs come down here to patronize anything or do any kind of business if they're risking their life? Good question. "You know," Mr.

Harrington said, shaking his head, "we need all this like a hole in the head."

I love the people of Detroit.

If I was ever going to operate a fully automatic machine gun in a combat zone again, my wish to God would be that my ammo bearer be an individual born and raised in Detroit.

I was a heavy weapons machine gunner in the infantry. Loved that job. Best job I ever had. When I was first put on "the gun," I was also issued a pistol, a Beretta 9mm. My understanding was that I was issued a pistol so that I'd have a weapon to fire in case my machine gun jammed. A good friend and brigade mate of mine, Spc. Horrocks, informed me of a different explanation for why a machine gunner in the infantry carries a pistol. He said that the real reason is so they have a weapon to threaten their ammo bearers with in case they get scared and get ideas of running away if they are being overrun. The Harringtons' position had been long ago overrun, and they have stood and fought.

•

We took a seat at the bar, and the cocktail waitress addressed him very formally as Mr. Harrington. He ordered a water, and I ordered a gin martini, straight up, and he told me that there has to be some kind of morality in this world, that his wife really believes in God, "I don't." He felt that we needed to learn how to live together. "Someone I once knew used to say we live on this spaceship earth," he told me, "and that we're all astronauts together."

This was probably the best martini I'd ever had at a bar. I liked being in Mr. Harrington's company on spaceship earth. I'd much rather have a drink with him than with any celebrity featured on TMZ.

He looked around the bar, then up at the ceiling, and told me about a police officer who came inside this bar once, got drunk, pulled his gun out, and started firing rounds up in the air. Maybe it's the futility of being a cop in Detroit; just too much after a while. We stood up and he brought me over to the elevator, and sure enough, three bullet holes, probably 9mm.

We took the elevator up, and he asked me if I'd like to take a look at some of the rooms on the top floor. There were two business suites, both of course empty and for lease. Everything was clean and modern. He showed me the bathroom and told me that during the election, Mrs. Obama stayed in this very room for a night. I looked at the toilet in awe: "Mrs. Obama took a shit on this toilet?" This was historic. I'm sure there are plenty of people out there who would love to purchase a toilet seat that our first lady once sat on, since that is absolutely the closest your ass is ever going to get to hers.

While staring out the window, I could see my building across the way. It was a disorienting vantage point, one to which I was entirely unaccustomed. These rooms were nice to visit, but they were not where I belonged.

As I gazed across at how my half lives—make that more like how my seven-eighths lives—Detroit came into stunning focus for me, and maybe the country, too. Metro Detroit really doesn't have a middle class. Here, you either have a lot, or you have nothing. The few are loaded, and everybody else lives like the people in my building, paycheck to paycheck, or no check to no check. I keep on hearing about a disappearing middle class in this country, but in Detroit it is not in the act of disappearing, it is gone.

Those who remain populate an increasingly barren landscape that once was one of the most fertile grounds of American wealth and ingenuity, and are now left to their own devices.

A country that no longer has a middle class.

My car has stopped working. I found out this lovely fact the next morning when I felt the need to leave town. I went to check up on it, to see if it was still there or if it had been towed. It responded with silence when I turned the key, and I saw that the back tires were now flat. Caliente, born in Detroit well before I came into this world, and here she will die.

CHAPTER TWENTY-ONE

Nothing Further

"In order to understand the world, one has to turn away from it on occasion."

ALBERT CAMUS

At Wayne County Airport, the terror alert level was "High," Orange. I was going on television, so my terror alert level was somewhat higher, but whenever I hear them announce the terror alert level at the airport, I hear that Fox News chime that they play whenever they have breaking news. I looked around to see if anybody else was concerned about the situation being Orange, which, if you think about it, is only one level away from "Severe," Red. Nobody seemed to be like, "You know what, I don't really think it's safe for me to be traveling right now with the world being Orange, I have a wife and kid. Fuck this, I'm going home. I'm going to wait till it goes back to Green, *maybe* Blue." One thing I thought for certain would happen after the election was that we'd get rid of all this silly terror alert level garbage, but sure enough, we still measure our fear on a color wheel.

A while ago I was interviewed by a music professor out in New York doing research for his book on soldiers and the music they listen to while serving in combat. Now published, he was working on press for its release. He contacted me, asking whether I'd like to be interviewed alongside him on a show on Fox News. I agreed, and shortly thereafter, the Fox News people contacted me, confirming that they'd pay for my round-trip ticket to New York City and car service to and from the airport, and put me up in a hotel for a night. All I had to do in return for them was a brief interview, and after that, I could return to the airport to fly back to Detroit, or wherever I wanted to go.

A free trip to New York is a free trip to New York. You can't really turn that down, right? But there's more to it than that. I also agreed to do this for my father, like an early Father's Day present. I could see my father watching me on Fox News, shedding a tear of immense pride, thinking to himself that yes, "My boy's finally made it."

My dad likes Fox News, he thinks they're "fair and balanced." My wife, on the other hand, can't stand Fox News. Won't watch it even for a second, and sincerely believes it to be the furthest thing from the news. "Entertainment." Since I've not had cable, thus, reception, for years, most recently not even owning a television, I didn't watch any network news until I moved into her place. Once I started to, whenever she would come home from a long day of work, turn on her television to find it on Fox News, she'd say things like, "What's wrong with my TV? Why is it that whenever I turn it on, it's always on Fox News? My television set never did this before!"

I watch Fox News not only to see what the other half of the country is thinking but perhaps for the same reasons why my mother used to watch soap operas. The quick cutting from one dramatic scene to the next does create a nice break from reality.

•

I flew Continental. When our plane began to descend, I looked out the window, and the world that we were about to land in looked colorful and pretty. All the houses were set nicely in rows, no burned-out shells of neighborhoods looking as though they had received heavy artillery fire. Homes painted in bright colors, clean streets, cars driving around, and all the factories looked operational. Newark, New Jersey, you are a jewel.

•

I walked past baggage claim with my black duffel in hand, and came across a Middle Eastern guy wearing a suit, holding a piece of white cardboard with my last name on it. As we were walking to the parking lot, he asked, "So how is business in Detroit, Mr. Buzzell?"

He must have addressed me as "Mister" because I like to travel light, but I sometimes like to dress up when I travel, as well. Though no one really does that anymore. I was now wearing my wool trench coat, suit and tie beneath, topped off with a fedora and my sunglasses. I replied, "Slow right now, but hopefully things will pick up soon."

"That's good."

I started feeling a little déjà vu in the back of his black car, remembering being on leave from Iraq. I had spent that time in New York City, and as the driver maneuvered through Manhattan, I was feeling that same sensory overload all over again.

Huge billboards, a sea of pedestrians, many well dressed, walking every which way, holding multiple shopping bags. And the buildings. All seemed inhabited and alive, the first floors operational retail stores, money being exchanged, a constant parade of consumers. Restaurants all open for business, on every sidewalk there were street vendors selling food—hot dogs, falafel, peanuts. People purchasing it, eating it, and loving it.

I felt a little woozy.

He dropped me off at my hotel, located in the middle of Times Square. The lobby was packed, many dressed to the nines; I imagined some being on their way to one of the few three-star Michelin-rated restaurants, having booked reservations months in advance.

I left my dark glasses on as I walked toward reception. As she pulled my reservation, the receptionist kindly asked, "Is this your first time staying with us, Mr. Buzzell?"

It was, but since there were people standing kind of close, well-dressed members of the same club, game face on, I told her, "No. I've stayed here several times before, you know, whenever the Waldorf is booked up."

With a smile, she handed me my door key and said, "Well, welcome back, Mr. Buzzell."

I smiled. "Thank you."

•

The room was nice, real nice, and after dropping my shit off, I quickly changed back into some street clothes and exited the hotel. I inhaled deeply and exhaled. I don't know what it is, but New York City has this certain smell that I can't really describe, and you can only smell it here.

Steam from the street vendors, air forcing itself up from the subway, the surrounding water, people, life; a unique smell. Just then, a lady took off her headphones and asked me if I knew directions to Seventh Avenue and Forty-sixth Street. I pointed her in the right direction.

I then stood for a second as people all around me walked by—without even noticing me standing there. I remember there used to be a time in my life when I tried to call this city home. No matter how hard I tried, it just never felt that way to me. Shortly after 9/11, I decided to leave. I moved back home to my parents' house. That no longer being an option made me feel more lost than ever. I shook that thought out of my head and started walking.

I used to live here, and when I did, I avoided Times Square as much as possible. Way too many people and tourists around these parts. Instead of taking the subway, I decided to just walk it, and on my walk through New York, I still couldn't believe how many people there were, all moving, some fast, some slow, and people doing stuff, whether it be eating outside at a café, or working a job doing construction, selling hot dogs, police officers on the street guiding traffic, bike messengers weaving in and out of cars, kamikaze cabdrivers competing for fares, vendors pushing their wares in and out of stores on dollies, women pushing baby strollers, men in suits, women in high heels, and over there, even a fashion photo shoot going on down a side street, people stopping to watch, eventually moving on to the crucial drama of their lives. I don't know what I expected or remembered, but living in Detroit had not prepared me for this.

It all reminded me again how I was once in love with this city. I then wondered if I could ever move back here. Probably not, for the same reasons why I decided not to go back to Iraq—I've already been there—why do it again? If I moved here, I'd wonder what else was out there and start feeling the pull to leave again. The same feeling I used to get every time I moved back home. I thought about this as I made my way.

I used to live out in Brooklyn. On Bedford Avenue. Not the Bedford Avenue located around the "hipster trolley" L train station, but the Bedford Avenue over by the Marcy Projects, over by where Jay-Z and Biggie grew up. Nice neighborhood. Really was.

When I lived blocks away from the Marcy PJ's, I used to grab my skateboard many a night and by myself skate down Bedford, through the Hassidic neighborhood all the way to Williamsburg, and when I got to the L train station, I'd quickly stop at the corner store, pick up a six-pack and smokes if need be, and after my purchase, exit and make a left heading west toward the direction of Manhattan, down N 7th Street. I'd take that all the way to the DEAD END sign.

The DEAD END sign is still there but the wooden pier off to the side that stretched beyond it, the one that was old, decrepit, and barely alive, is not.

Posted on the chain-link fence was a NO TRESPASSING sign which I'd ignore and I'd walk out onto the pier all the way to the end, by myself, sit down, light up a smoke, open up a bottle, and just sit there under the stars drinking while staring off at the Manhattan skyline. The lights radiated from the city and those two ominous tall towers that stood there side by side over by Wall Street.

It was peaceful and I used to love hearing the sound of that bottle splashing every time I finished one and threw it out as far as I could into the East River. Then I'd open up another bottle and sit there and continue drinking. I also remember how I used to sit there and think to myself how there had to be more to life than this, but had no idea what in the hell that was so in the meantime, I'd figure I'd just sit around and wait.

For a while doing this became a part of my routine. Two or three times a week I'd go out there to that pier, sometimes for hours. At night, every time, I'd be the only one there and it made me feel like the loneliest person on earth. Here I am living near and around a city of millions and here I am, the only person doing this.

Don't know what happened to it, but the last time I was here and decided to walk down memory lane while holding a six-pack, when I came to the DEAD END sign I sadly discovered that the pier beyond the fence was completely gone.

Everything else appeared to be the same except the professional-looking signs posted all around indicating new high-rise condos to be developed sometime in the near future.

Since that pier is no longer there, I make it a point to go to this particular bar every time I go back to New York. I'm scared to death, like the pier, of someday coming back and finding it no longer there,* what with all the redevel-

---

* Which will eventually be the case since they recently announced that they will be closing their doors.

opment that's been going on around that neighborhood
the last several years—the new upscale condos, the Whole
Foods behemoth a block away, etc. CBGB was once around
the corner, but that's become a museum piece in Vegas;
luxe restaurants and John Varvatos have moved in.

When I stepped inside the bar, I was relieved that it
hadn't changed much at all—still a dive, still dark, still a
shit hole loaded with drunks, still the way I like it. "Let's
Get Fucked Up" by The Cramps still on the jukebox. I took
a seat at the end of the bar, and once I finished my shot and
a drink, I stepped back outside for a smoke break.

It then hit me: I'd made it. I'd made it all the way across
the country.

The last time I was here, in this bar, a guy wearing
a parka and Yankees hat asked me if I was interested in
any "party favors." I was, so I bought an eight ball off
him, did a couple bumps in the bathroom, and since I
was about to board the train from Grand Central to D.C.
on my way to Obama's inauguration, I figured there'd
be cops and sniffing dogs crawling all over the place, so
I gave the rest of what I had to the bar back. We'd had
a nice chat that evening, and I remembered the time a
while back when he had crushed up some Valium that we
shared in the bathroom. When I told him I was on my
way to the inauguration, he asked, arms folded, "What
for?" I told him to witness history, and he seemed unimpressed. "Don't get me wrong, Obama is a good morale
boost for our country, and I think we need that right now,
that's good. But people are fucking stupid, nothing's going
to change, people still aren't going to do shit and it's going

to be the same shit, only now Obama's fault. Watch, nothing will change. Nothing." And when he told me this, I remember thinking, "What a shitty attitude to have. I want my fucking coke back!" But maybe the bar back was right.

I thought of all this while smoking outside the bar, as life went on. People walked by, some by themselves, some in couples, some in groups. As cabs drove by, drinks were being poured and consumed inside the bar, as well as every other bar across the country, and world. A couple pushing a stroller passed by.

.

People have told me that as soon as their kid was born, their life changed, how they "just knew," and how they all had some kind of realization, or something like that, about their purpose in life, their plot. Some have asked if I've had some kind of similar epiphany with the birth of my son. I can honestly say no, I haven't, and honestly, I think that's a lot of weight to put on the little guy.

All that really happened to me when he was born was me thinking, "Holy shit. He looks just like me." This kind of scared the hell out of me, though it did eliminate any potential doubt that I was the father, if there was any, which there wasn't.

After the doctors handed me a pair of steel scissors for the honor of cutting the bloody umbilical cord, setting him free from his mother, they took him off to the side to clean him off. Shortly after, they called me over.

A look of horror spread across my wife's face as the doctors informed us all, "Not to be alarmed," but that he was having a difficult time breathing due to fluid in his lungs, and that they were going to take him into the intensive care unit next door. He also had jaundice, which I had also had when I was born.

As Mom went into recovery, I followed the doctors next door to the ICU, where they placed him inside a tiny baby hospital bed, surrounded by preemies and a bunch of other babies dealt a bad card upon arrival. I stood there uncomfortably next to him, feeling awkward as I just stared at him, not knowing what to do, or what to say: What do you say to a newborn? "Hey, how's it going, I'm your father— hey, stop crying, it's not that bad. I didn't get to choose mine either. Yeah, this sucks, I know, but once the doctors here get you all good to go, we're outta here and you can be back with Mommy again."

He looked terrified. If my mother were there with me, she'd probably yell at me, "Do something!" My father got that a lot from her, as well, so I did. I kind of stuck my index finger out for him, and with his tiny, tiny fingers he instantly grabbed it and stopped crying for a second as he held on tight, real tight, and did not let go. As I watched, the nurses came by to shove an IV into his arm, sticking him with needles, one right after another. He cried, all the while still holding on to my finger.

I felt sorry for him—what a crummy way to start your life off, first being introduced to me, and then all this. Poor kid.

It was a bit surreal for me to all of a sudden go from hanging out inside hospitals witnessing my mother die a very painful death to, almost overnight, being thrown into the hospital to now witness the joy of bringing a new life, which I helped create, into the world.

When the nurses started taping monitoring devices and tubes to him, I remembered how my mother, while doped out on pain medication, would rebelliously yank all the IVs and cords from her arms, with a look of satisfaction on her face that things were going to be her way or no way.

Now my tiny son did the same, defiantly yanking them from his tiny body. This kid is 100 percent my son. I smiled, chuckling. I love him.

The story goes that when my wife was all fixed up and they wheeled her in from her recovery room, I was seated on a chair next to his bed, passed out from exhaustion, his hand still tightly wound around my finger.

•

Previous generations tuned out by running away, further from whatever was going on in their lives. Though it's tempting, and I fully understand the reasons why—hell, I've done it—I wonder if you could do the opposite, tune out and dive headfirst into whatever was coming at you. For me, the direction of my son. Focus on that.

•

My mother passed in March, and so in May, for Mother's Day, I visited her grave site. I went by myself, and since she liked flowers, I had some with me. I never really noticed or paid any attention to flowers at all until after she passed away. Now I can't help but notice them every time I see them. When I was going through old photos of her, they all seemed to include flowers. I had some roses with me, which I stuck into the ground above her grave, along with a Mother's Day card.

I hung out at the cemetery for a while. Several others were there that day as well. I talked to my mother for what felt like the first time ever, and while thinking how much has changed since the last Mother's Day, I got depressed, really depressed. The Mother's Day before this she was fine, in great health. She had just run Bay to Breakers for the first time, and with no preparation beforehand, finishing the race by repeating the mantra, "If he can do it, and she can do it, then why not me?"

Months later, weak, her hair nearly completely gone from chemo, assisted by a cane and my father, she'd get up on the elliptical machine at the gym. Just as she had done every morning for years, it was her daily routine, she'd stay on that machine until her thirty minutes was up, putting forth her best effort, not once letting the cancer defeat her, disregarding the flashing "Pause" and "Pedal Faster" messages.

That fight-to-the-death spirit and "If he can do it, and she can do it, then why not me" confidence—something I've never had—is something I want my son to have. I wanted to pass it on to him by doing what my mother did, leading by example.

She never smoked and hardly ever drank, maybe once or twice during the holidays, but never more than a glass or two of wine. Except for that one time in Cancún on the Club Med vacation with my father when she got ripped on the free booze.

I don't know how I did this, especially when my father

called me several times in advance to remind me, but I forgot Mother's Day the year before she died. It completely slipped my mind. I didn't even know that Mother's Day had passed until the day after, when my father called me up to inform me that I had fucked that one up, how I should have sent flowers, a card, something, even calling and talking to her would have been nice. I remember just saying sorry, and how I would remember next Mother's Day.

So there I was, visiting my mother, flowers and card on the day I remembered. I slowly walked back to BART, where I stared out the window on my way back home. Once the train moved underground, everything turned black and I was able to see my reflection in the window; I looked away.

My mother always reminded me to smile; she never felt I smiled enough. This is one of the things I've learned to do a lot of after losing my mother, especially after my son was born. When he was born, I saw how my wife was with him, how excited our families were to be with him. For my family, unspoken sadness in the absence of my mother. Thinking of her, I understand now; I want my son to smile, I want him to be happy.

•

I don't ever recall a night spent in New York City where I didn't end it totally wasted, but tonight I just didn't feel like doing that. My thoughts dwelled heavily on the fact that you can never go back home again, but, more optimistically, you can build a new home, that things are never really that bad. Yes, they could always be worse, but we get through it. People are resilient, good things happen.

Instead of going back inside the bar, I flicked my cigarette out. Then I started walking.

·

Heading back home, my carry-on filled with cold-cut sandwiches taken from the green room, I sat in my seat, thinking about home, and what it meant to me at this point. The
airline stewardess came around and asked me whether I'd
like a drink. I thought about it, and told her no.

"I'm fine, thank you." And I smiled.

ACKNOWLEDGMENTS

Julia Barrett
Tyler Cabot
Isaac Callahan
Julia Cheiffetz
David Granger
Peter Hansen
The Harringtons
Mother of my child
My family
Cesar M. Ramos
Katie Salisbury
Heather Schroder
Nicole Tourtelot
Mark Warren

Everybody else who helped out and made this happen.

ABOUT THE AUTHOR

Colby Buzzell is the author of *My War: Killing Time in Iraq* and served as an infantryman in the United States Army during the Iraq War. Assigned to a Stryker Brigade Combat Team in 2003, Buzzell blogged from the front lines of Iraq as a replacement for his habitual journaling back in the States. In 2004 Buzzell was profiled in *Esquire*'s "Best and Brightest" issue and has since contributed frequently to the magazine. *The Washington Post* referred to his article, "Digging a Hole All the Way to America" as "A Tour de Force Travelogue" and in 2010 his article "Down & Out In Fresno and San Francisco" was selected for *The Best American Travel Writing 2010*. His work has also appeared in the *San Francisco Chronicle* and on *This American Life*. He currently lives in San Francisco, California, and has no plans whatsoever of staying there.